365 Things GOD Wants You to Know

Christine A. Dallman

 Publications International, Ltd.

P9-DZY-957

Christine A. Dallman is a freelance writer living near Everett, Washington. She is the author of *Daily Devotions for Seniors,* an inspirational resource for maturing adults, as well as coauthor of several other Publications International, Ltd., titles.

Cover photo: © Sharon K. Broutzas

Louis Weber, CEO
Publications International, Ltd.
7373 North Cicero Avenue
Lincolnwood, Illinois 60712

ISBN-13: 978-1-4508-3017-1
ISBN-10: 1-4508-3017-X

Manufactured in USA.

8 7 6 5 4 3 2 1

God's Love for Us
Is Enduring and Awesome

Welcome to *365 Things God Wants You to Know*—a
versatile little volume that offers important truths
for readers of all ages and stages of spiritual growth.
For those unfamiliar with the Bible, this book brings
a great deal of information to the table that will
enlighten and encourage your budding faith. For
those more familiar with the Scriptures, the daily
affirmations contained on each page will come as a
reminder to strengthen an already established faith.
And for each reader, there is the raw power of the
Word of God itself that will bring its timeless inspi-
ration to nourish your spirit in every way.

As you read the meditations in *365 Things God Wants
You to Know,* you'll discover that each daily reading
is brief—only about one hundred words—containing
a passage of Scripture along with spiritual insights.
This again is part of the book's great versatility, as it
can serve either as your sole daily devotional reading or as a supplement to other reading material.
You can read the daily entries—one for each day of
the year—by yourself or in a group or family setting;
you can read them at mealtime or at bedtime, as a

pick-me-up while waiting in line or as an emergency measure of encouragement "in the thick of things." The possibilities are wide and wonderful.

Finally, as you consider the content of a book that would be so bold as to call itself *365 Things God Wants You to Know*, there must be the assurance that each entry bears the clear message of Scripture—what God has truly told us in his Word. That is the aim of this book. Of course, a publication of this size and scope can't contain *all* of God's assurances and promises, but you'll find a rich representation of what the Scriptures reveal—important truths that have guided and sustained men and women of faith from the earliest times.

As you read, meditate on, and absorb each truth within this book, you will be strengthened in your relationship with God. The things he wants you to know are for your benefit as his beloved child. His love fills his instruction, overflows in his assurances, and saturates his promises. And, despite any other ideas we might have about what we think God wants us to know, the prevailing theme we discover is his great love for us. May that love surround and sustain you as you take time each day to read and receive it anew.

God values you. God's Word brims with life-giving affirmations—things he wants you to know. What kind of *things*? Here's one that's very important. Jesus tells us that God is so engaged with his creation that he values even the little birds he's made. And yet, "You are of more value than many sparrows," Jesus assures us (Luke 12:7). God knows everything about us. He could tell you the exact number of hairs on your head right now. Imagine, then, how much he cares about the deeper realities of your life—about what makes you who you are.

God hears your prayers. With so much praying going on in the world, you may wonder, *Does God really hear my prayers?* In Psalm 4:3, the psalmist didn't have a doubt: "Know that the Lord has set apart the faithful for himself; the Lord hears when I call to him." It's a comfort to know that the God of the universe is not too busy or distracted to attentively bend his ear toward us. Jesus told his followers, "Ask, and it will be given you; search, and you will find; knock, and the door will be opened for you" (Luke 11:9). So, pray away! God *is* listening.

God grants wisdom. Did you know that God is happy to give you wisdom when you need it? Listen to this promise: "If any of you is lacking in wisdom, ask God, who gives to all generously and ungrudgingly, and it will be given you" (James 1:5). This offer has only one condition: that you ask in faith, not doubting his promise. Do you have a big decision to make, a difficult dilemma to solve, or an interpersonal impasse? Ask God for the wisdom you need. Then trust. It might not arrive in a way you expect, but it'll come. Just wait and see.

God is always with you. Whether it's commuting to work, having coffee with friends, taking a favorite walk, or even sleeping soundly through the night—whatever it is, wherever you are, God wants you to know that he's there with you. He's the friend who always has time, never moves to another part of the world, is forever ready to listen, and provides the best counsel. It's just a matter of realizing he's there. "And remember," Jesus said, "I am with you always, to the end of the age" (Matthew 28:20). Matthew closed his Gospel with those words—words well worth holding onto.

God wants to adopt you. Here's a mind-blowing truth that God wants you to know: He, the God of the universe, wants to adopt you as his own child. It's true! "See what love the Father has given us, that we should be called children of God." (1 John 3:1). The Apostle Paul affirmed, "When we cry, 'Abba! Father!' it is that very Spirit [of adoption] bearing witness with our spirit that we are children of God" (Romans 8:15–16). There's no better father than God, and his gracious offer to adopt us into his family is open to all.

God gives abundant life. When it comes to life in God's kingdom, there's something God wants you to realize. Jesus said, "I came that they may have life, and have it abundantly" (John 10:10). So whenever books and movies portray the life of faith as square and stilted, out of touch and drab, remember that's not how God intends life with him at all. Real life with him is not a boring, trackless waste of dreariness. It's a day-to-day adventure filled with the light and life of heaven in our hearts—a life truly worth living.

Faith pleases God. God wants you to know that your faith in him makes him glad. In fact, the writer of Hebrews tells us, "Without faith it is impossible to please God, for whoever would approach him must believe that he exists and that he rewards those who seek him" (11:6). It's not our accomplishments, money, talents, or things that give God pleasure. What he loves is our willingness to live in trusting relationship with him. In turn, he affirms our faith by sending his blessings to encourage us on our way. The truth is, your trust-filled heart pleases him even as you read this.

God offers you rest. "Come to me," Jesus said, "all you that are weary and are carrying heavy burdens, and I will give you rest. Take my yoke upon you, and learn from me.... For my yoke is easy, and my burden is light" (Matthew 11:28–30). God wants you to know that you don't have to carry your burdens on your own. He knows our strength is finite, and he tenderly accommodates our need for rest. In fact, he offers to be our source of rest and strength, whenever we're willing to come to him and receive it.

God forgives completely. Take a moment and let these words sink in: "For as the heavens are high above the earth, so great is his steadfast love toward those who fear him; as far as the east is from the west, so far he removes our transgressions from us" (Psalm 103:11–12). If you turn your face due east and begin walking in that direction, you will never (without turning around) face the west. In that sense, east never meets west, and neither does God in his mercy ever revisit what he's forgiven.

God is like a gentle shepherd. In a serene, pastoral metaphor, the psalmist describes God as our keeper: "The Lord is my shepherd, I shall not [be in] want. He makes me lie down in green pastures; he leads me beside still waters" (Psalm 23:1–2). The image is of a tender-hearted guardian, who finds the best possible ways to care for his beloved sheep. Green pastures are soft, cool, and nourishing, while still waters quench thirst without any of the dangers of a swift current. God is looking after you with just this kind of gentle, watchful love.

In God there's freedom. Civil liberties are wonderful. A healthy mind and body is a blessing. Relationships that allow us to thrive are lovely. But even if freedom eludes you in some of these areas, God wants you to know that there's a deep spiritual freedom that can be yours—a freedom that no outer circumstance can confine or fetter. God himself is its source, for "the Lord is the Spirit, and where the Spirit of the Lord is, there is freedom" (2 Corinthians 3:17). You can enjoy it fully—a strong, invulnerable freedom—as you grow in your relationship with him.

God's protection surrounds your life. "The angel of the Lord encamps around those who fear him, and delivers them" (Psalm 34:7). Imagine it: an unseen angel "setting up camp" wherever you are. Angels not only act as God's messengers but also as heaven's army that fights against our enemy the devil, his minions, and all their plans. Sometimes God may permit certain things to happen in our lives, but we can be sure it's not because some angel missed God's cue, but rather because God is doing something important for our greater good.

The creation speaks of God. Have you ever tried communicating without words? Musicians, dancers, painters, and actors (using nonverbal skills) do this very thing. Without words, the natural world around us is part of God's own self-expression. "The heavens are telling the glory of God," said the psalmist, "and the firmament proclaims his handiwork. Day to day pours forth speech, and night to night declares knowledge.... Their voice is not heard; yet their voice goes out ... to the end of the world" (Psalm 19:1–4). That's why discovering more about our Lord God can be as near as your next venture outdoors.

You can trust God to meet your needs. As you follow God's lead in life, you can know without a doubt that he's going to provide all that you need along the way. Even today, as you lift your prayers to him, you can take hold of these trust-filled words written by the Apostle Paul two millennia ago: "My God will fully satisfy every need of yours according to his riches in glory in Christ Jesus" (Philippians 4:19)—words that are every bit as true today because

God is still in the business of providing for his children.

God knows how to restore you. Things can get broken in life, and not just physical possessions. Our hearts can get broken, our souls can become damaged, and our spirits can suffer harm. But there's good news for us whenever our inner person needs mending. King David said it succinctly as he spoke of the Lord's power to heal in Psalm 23:3: "He restores my soul." It's a brief statement that can be easily passed over, but to linger over it is to allow the unfurling of great hope for wholeness—hope that fuels our faith as God remakes us within.

God's Word brings wisdom. Opening the Scriptures is like entering a gold mine. The writer of Psalm 19 praised the Lord's instruction: "The decrees of the Lord are sure, making wise the simple;...the commandment of the Lord is clear, enlightening the eyes.... More to be desired are they than gold, even much fine gold" (verses 7–8, 10). Of course, the Bible's a big volume, so if you're looking for a place to begin digging, check out the "wisdom literature" books of Psalms and Proverbs.

Our help comes from God. When we're in a fix, we look for a helping hand. Sometimes we can count on a family member or a friend to come to our aid. But then there are those times when no earthly help is available. What then? The writer of Psalm 121 knew where to turn: "I lift up my eyes to the hills—from where will my help come? My help comes from the Lord, who made heaven and earth" (verses 1–2). God offers his help to you 24/7, from big crises to little problems and everything in between.

God helps the humble. People who care about others are grateful for the gift of life. They humbly understand that they need God without even thinking about it. They're so busy enjoying what makes others wonderful that they don't envy or compete. While well acquainted with their own flaws and weaknesses, they don't focus on them. Instead, they confide in God, trusting him to help. In response,

"[God] leads the humble in what is right, and teaches the humble his way" (Psalm 25:9). True humility moves God to meet us where we're at as he leads us where we need to go.

God loves what's right. Classic heroes of comic book fame fight against corruption and evil in defense of what's right. Wouldn't it be nice to have a hero like that to come to your rescue? Consider this passage from Psalm 45: "Gird your sword on your thigh, O mighty one.... In your majesty ride on victoriously for the cause of truth and to defend the right.... Your throne, O God, endures for ever and ever. Your royal scepter is a scepter of equity; you love righteousness and hate wickedness" (verses 3–4, 6–7). Need a hero? God's the true hero!

God's angels help us. The Bible tells of angels intervening in human events. Angels brought messages to Abraham, Mary, Zechariah, and others. They rescued Lot from a burning city and Daniel from the mouths of lions. They served meals to Elijah and fed Jesus after his temptation. You may wonder, *Do angels still intervene in our lives today?* The writer of Hebrews answers that question with a rhetorical one: "Are not all angels spirits in the divine service, sent to serve for the sake of those who are to inherit salvation?" (1:14). Yes, though often unseen, the work of angels on our behalf is still ongoing.

God custom-designed you. A slogan that was popular a few decades ago was grammatically messed up, but it was right in every other way. It went something like this: "God made me, and God don't make junk." If you're a poetic soul, you can find this truth stated a bit more eloquently in Psalm 139:13–14: "For it was you who formed my inward parts; you knit me together in my mother's womb. I praise you, for I am fearfully and wonderfully made." Indeed, God made you, and he did a fantastic job. Never doubt it!

God blesses the spiritually hungry. "Blessed are the poor in spirit," Jesus said, "for theirs is the kingdom of heaven" (Matthew 5:3). That's wonderful news for those of us who have spiritual hunger, who sense our need for God, and who long for him to open our eyes to truth. For though we are poor in spirit, God blesses us with the promise that we will be permanent residents in his heavenly kingdom. Meanwhile, the Lord plants the seed of salvation in our hearts until we finally realize its fullness in our heavenly home.

God blesses the hurting. Jesus said, "Blessed are those who mourn, for they will be comforted" (Matthew 5:4). While life's pains come in a wide range of shapes and sizes, depths and durations, God fully comprehends each trial we encounter. His concern for us, however, goes beyond mere comprehension. God comes to us with profound compassion, ministering comfort we might not have thought possible. Though God is patient and tender in his approach, we sometimes don't recognize God's work in our hearts at first; but in time, we come to realize the full blessing of his comforting care.

God blesses the meek. Jesus said, "Blessed are the meek, for they will inherit the earth" (Matthew 5:5). But *what on earth* does it mean to *inherit the earth?* Well, it can be said that people who go through life loving God and "doing unto others" are folks who walk humbly, enjoying his approval. They put themselves in a position to receive from God whatever he sees fit to give them—anything on the face of the earth. As God's children, they are blessed as heirs of all he owns—and he owns it all!

God blesses the upright. Jesus said, "Blessed are those who hunger and thirst for righteousness, for they will be filled" (Matthew 5:6). A deep desire for righteousness has two parts: One part is about desiring to *do what's right;* the other part has to do with a longing to *see right prevail* in the world around us. Whenever you crave what is right and true and good, you demonstrate the hunger Jesus talked about. Rest assured: There's coming a day when that hunger will be satisfied—when the blessing of God's righteous kingdom will be fully established.

God blesses the merciful. Jesus said, "Blessed are the merciful, for they will receive mercy" (Matthew 5:7). Mercy is something we all love to receive when we need it. The difficult part of mercy is when others need it from us. Depending on the situation, extending mercy can be inconvenient, costly, risky, and/or downright painful at times. But when we let mercy win the day in our interactions with others, we personally identify with the mercy Jesus has shown us. In doing so, we invite the blessing of God's mercy into our lives.

God blesses purity. Jesus said to his listeners, "Blessed are the pure in heart, for they will see God" (Matthew 5:8). When something is pure, there's nothing mixed in to dilute or compromise it. Our hearts can have such pureness when we seek to please God first and foremost. For example, when Jesus chose his disciples, he said about a man named Nathanael, "Here is truly an Israelite in whom there is no deceit!" (John 1:47). Interestingly, Nathanael, who had just met Jesus, immediately recognized Jesus as the Son of God! Nathanael's pure heart allowed him to clearly see Jesus for who he truly is.

God blesses the peaceful. Jesus said, "Blessed are the peacemakers, for they will be called children of God" (Matthew 5:9). It seems that there's one in every family—the mom or dad, sister or brother who tries really hard to move everyone toward a peaceful resolution when conflict arises. To seek the path of peace is a reflection of God's own heart of reconciliation. When our children or protégés emulate us in good ways, we say joyfully, "That's my girl!" or "That's my boy!" Similarly, God is delighted to call us his children when we seek the path of peace.

God blesses perseverance. Jesus said, "Blessed are those who are persecuted for righteousness' sake, for theirs is the kingdom of heaven" (Matthew 5:10). At times it takes true grit to stand firm in your faith. When doing the right thing is unpopular, when forgoing gossip or "office politics" leaves you on the outside, when people deride your moral convictions, you may be left feeling alienated and lonely. The temptation is to make the difficulty go away by convincing your conscience to take a different stance. But there's no blessing in that, only regret. Be encouraged and stay the course; it leads heavenward.

Your life flavors the world around you. "You are the salt of the earth," Jesus said to his followers (Matthew 5:13). There were relatively few disciples to begin with, but of course, a little salt goes a long way. Eventually the gospel reached around the entire globe, and the "seasoning" of those first disciples flavors our lives even today. In turn, our faith flavors the world around us. The right choices you make, the kindnesses you show, and the worthy conversations you have—these kinds of things bring the seasoning of Christ's love into your interpersonal relationships.

Your life lights up the world around you. "You are the light of the world," Jesus said. "...No one after lighting a lamp puts it under the bushel basket, but on the lampstand, and it gives light to all in the house. In the same way, let your light shine before others" (Matthew 5:14–16). Light doesn't make noise, but it's impossible to miss as it scatters the darkness. Similarly, you don't have to make a lot of noise about your faith. It will clearly make itself known when you boldly shine the light of God's love all around you.

God wants us to love our enemies. "Love your enemies," Jesus continued to teach his followers, "do good to those who hate you, bless those who curse you, pray for those who abuse you" (Luke 6:27–28). Gulp! That's a really tall order. But here's how we can find the heart to fill Jesus' command: "God proves his love for us," Paul said, "in that while we still were sinners Christ died for us" (Romans 5:8). When we remember that God reached out to us at our worst and loved us, we can pay it forward to our enemies, showing them the same love that changed our own lives. When we do, we are not only obeying our Lord's command but also spreading his love.

God wants us to forgive others. When Jesus taught his disciples to pray, he included these words: "Forgive us our debts, as we also have forgiven our debtors" (Matthew 6:12). After concluding the prayer, he explained, "For if you forgive others their trespasses, your heavenly Father will also forgive you" (verse 14). Without a doubt, the quickest route to letting go of the "debts" that are owed us is to recall the ones God has forgiven us. When we're able to forgive others, we can enjoy the freedom of having fully embraced God's forgiveness for us.

You can pray simply. The prospect of praying can be intimidating, especially when someone's just getting used to the idea. There's good news, though. There is no one language God requires us to use. In fact, Jesus reminds us to keep it simple: "When you are praying, do not heap up empty phrases as [some do]; for they think that they will be heard because of their many words" (Matthew 6:7-8). God just wants honest, open conversation with us. We can speak to him as we would a friend or a beloved parent, for he is both.

Things of true value are eternal. "Store up for yourselves treasures in heaven, where neither moth nor rust consumes and where thieves do not break in and steal" (Matthew 6:20). With these words, Jesus urges us to invest ourselves in things that matter for eternity. But what are these things? Someone once noted that the only things on earth that will last forever are God's Word, people, and the things we do to honor God. Well, that's a short list, but it holds great potential for the most meaningful kinds of investments.

God takes care of you. "Do not worry about your life," Jesus continued to teach. "Is not life more than food, and the body more than clothing?... But strive first for the kingdom of God and his righteousness, and all these things will be given to you as well" (Matthew 6:25, 33). "Do not worry about anything," Paul concurred, "but... let your requests be made known to God. And the peace of God... will guard your hearts and your minds in Christ Jesus" (Philippians 4:6–7). Always remember, God's got your back.

The Golden Rule is God's rule. Jesus put all the teaching of God's law and his prophets into this verbal nutshell: "In everything do to others as you would have them do to you" (Matthew 7:12). Whoever dubbed it the Golden Rule understood its immense value. While it's true that there are older teachings in Eastern wisdom literature that speak of *not* doing to others what we would not want done to us, Jesus pushed the stakes higher. He goes beyond not harming others to actively working in their best interest at all times. It's our challenge to "go for the gold" and treat others with sincere kindness.

God rewards generosity. "Give, and it will be given to you," Jesus said, "...for the measure you give will be the measure you get back" (Luke 6:38). Far from advocating the idea of giving just to get back, Jesus was revealing God's heart toward us when we're open-handed with others. Generosity begins with God giving us enough to share, and it ends with him blessing us for being willing to share. It's been said many times, and it's true: "We can't out-give God."

Jesus' teachings are rock solid. It's not easy making our way through life. So many philosophies, so many books, and so many opinions! But above the din, Jesus raises his voice and reminds us that he is the source of rock-solid truth. "Everyone then who hears these words of mine and acts on them," he said, "will be like a wise man who built his house on rock. The rain fell, the floods came, and the winds blew and beat on that house, but it did not fall" (Matthew 7:24–25). Now that's a foundation—one to bank your life on.

God's Spirit will guide us. All the stress goes out of navigating unknown territory when you have a guide. The guide knows all the best places to go, the shortcuts, the scenic routes, and the places to avoid. For our guide in life, God has given us his Spirit. The unknown future lies before us at every moment, but it is not unknown to God. His Spirit will lead us if we'll accept his guidance. "If we live by the Spirit," Paul said, "let us also be guided by the Spirit" (Galatians 5:25). Follow God's Spirit, and you can't go wrong.

God's Spirit produces love. Try as we might, we often don't love as well we'd like to. Of course, only God's love is perfect, so it's his love we need if we are going to love consistently and selflessly. That's precisely why God sent his Spirit to be our helper. His presence with us and within us is the source of the love we need. As you learn to keep in step with the Spirit, you'll recognize God's love flowing through you more and more, for "the fruit of the Spirit is love..." (Galatians 5:22).

God's Spirit produces joy. "The fruit of the Spirit is...joy," we also read in Galatians 5:22. Spirit-cultivated joy comes from the delighted confidence we have in God. It sprouts and flourishes as God's Spirit helps us focus on God's goodness in our daily walk with him. As a result, this joy quite naturally spills over from within us into our words and actions, coloring our character and our very demeanor. It's something other people may even notice and want to know more about—a great opportunity for you to point them to the source of your joy.

God's Spirit produces peace. Peace begins in our hearts. If we lack peace within, we'll be hard-pressed to find a situation or circumstance that doesn't feel frustrating or unsettling. It's good to know, then, that we can experience and enjoy inner peace as we walk with God's Spirit, for "the fruit of the Spirit is...peace" (Galatians 5:22). Paul also urged, "Let the peace of Christ rule in your hearts, to which indeed you were called" (Colossians 3:15). Such a call reveals God's kind intentions toward us as his Spirit leads us along. God's peace, as it dwells within us, is good not only for us but for the body of Christ as well.

God's Spirit produces patience. It's been said in jest, "Never pray for patience!" The joke is that doing so would invite all sorts of trials for working the desired quality into our character. Fortunately, there's a better way to grow in patience, and that is, learning that "the fruit of the Spirit is...patience" (Galatians 5:22). God's Spirit cultivates true patience in our hearts, helping us become "quick to listen, slow to speak, slow to anger" (James 1:19). We also learn to wait for God's direction instead of running ahead on our own. The net result: less stress all the way around.

God's Spirit produces kindness. Kindness is an underrated power. Think about it: Has anyone's kind word or gesture ever changed the course of your day by lifting your spirits or getting your mind running in a more positive track? A kind response to someone who is frustrated and angry can change that person's demeanor in a moment. Truly, "a soft answer turns away wrath" (Proverbs 15:1). Why is kindness so powerful? Because it's God's way: "the fruit of the Spirit is . . . kindness" (Galatians 5:22). Let God show you where you can insert a kind word or deed today.

God's Spirit produces generosity. Generosity is most often linked to the idea of a benevolent soul freely disbursing money or gifts. But generosity has many faces. A child giving away her last piece of candy when it was her favorite flavor is generous. Taking time to buy a panhandler something to eat is generous. Listening patiently to a neighbor's concerns (though you've heard them before) is generous. "The fruit of the Spirit is... generosity" (Galatians 5:22), and as generosity grows in our hearts, it reveals the good work of God's Spirit there.

God's Spirit produces faithfulness. "Many proclaim themselves loyal, but who can find one worthy of trust?" (Proverbs 20:6). Sometimes we feel just like that—like it's hard to find anyone who cares much about being true. But thankfully, even if everyone else lets us down, *God* is still faithful. And since "the fruit of the Spirit is... faithfulness" (Galatians 5:22), we can be faithful too. As integrity, honesty, reliability, and honor increase in our character, we will certainly see God's Spirit at work within us, producing the fruit of faithfulness.

God's Spirit produces gentleness. What is gentleness? A breeze is gentle compared to a gust. A hug is gentle compared to a kick in the shins. A purring kitten is gentle compared to a savage lion. Gentleness in our lives has a quiet, tender quality—one of compassion and empathy, helping us understand how it feels to be treated one way instead of another. "The fruit of the Spirit is ... gentleness" (Galatians 5:22–23), and it's God's Spirit who helps us discern the path of gentleness as we interact with others.

God's Spirit produces self-control. Here's the last item on the list of spiritual fruit: "self-control" (Galatians 5:23). Wait! Don't turn the page! This is a message of hope. The good news is that when we invite God's Spirit to work in and through us, he begins to do in us what we could never do through our own efforts. And in the process, God is patient with us. He is faithful to see us through. He is able to give us everything we need, especially self-control, to find the freedom we long for.

Choosing wise friends is wise. Proverbs is a treasure trove of wise instruction and memorable maxims. For example, consider this scriptural insight: "Whoever walks with the wise becomes wise, but the companion of fools suffers harm" (Proverbs 13:20). While it's not rocket science, it's a true assessment of the power friends can wield in our life, influencing our very thoughts and actions. So the bottom line: Choosing our closest friends is an exercise in choosing our own character development. And because God loves us, he wants us to be discerning about whom we choose to walk beside us on this path of life.

God can make things good again. There are times when we might feel as if we've messed things up in life beyond all hope. But God is in the business of redemption—of taking messed-up situations and people and restoring them. It's like a home makeover show where an unlivable space is transformed into a lovely habitation. "We know that all things work together for good for those who love God," Paul assures us, "who are called according to his purpose" (Romans 8:28). There's always hope when God is in the house.

Well-chosen words are wise. In the Book of Proverbs, God has a lot to say about what comes out of our mouths. Take some time to ponder the following proverbs: "Pleasant words are like a honeycomb, sweetness to the soul and health to the body" (16:24). "Rash words are like sword thrusts, but the tongue of the wise brings healing" (12:18). "One who spares words is knowledgeable; one who is cool in spirit has understanding" (17:27). And lastly, a truly insightful proverb: "A word fitly spoken is like apples of gold in a setting of silver" (25:11). May your words be fitly spoken!

Accepting God's discipline is wise. The "D" word can be scary if we think it's all about punishment, but the discipline that comes from our heavenly Father is not about that. His discipline is about helping us stay on track so we don't end up lost—or worse. His motive is pure love for us: "My child, do not despise the Lord's discipline or be weary of his reproof, for the Lord reproves the one he loves, as a father the son in whom he delights" (Proverbs 3:11–12). The Lord wants us to know that he disciplines us because he cares about our character in the same way parents care for the character of their child.

Honoring parents is wise. In Ephesians 6:2–3, Paul wrote, "'Honor your father and mother'—this is the first commandment with a promise—'so that it may be well with you and you may live long on the earth.'" That's a weighty and wonderful promise! Even in adulthood, we can find ways to honor (if they are still with us) those who raised us. It's gratifying—even if there's a difficult situation—to rise above the difficulty and let God's love prevail.

Preparing for the future is wise. While we cannot know the future, it's wise to prepare as best we can for it. So here's an important caveat: "Go to the ant,... consider its ways, and be wise... [I]t prepares its food in summer, and gathers its sustenance in harvest" (Proverbs 6:6, 8). God encourages us to think ahead, always consulting with him about what needs to be done. It's not wise to act as if we are

God's robots, dismissing any responsibility for our own lives.

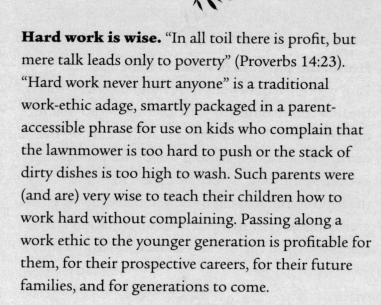

Hard work is wise. "In all toil there is profit, but mere talk leads only to poverty" (Proverbs 14:23). "Hard work never hurt anyone" is a traditional work-ethic adage, smartly packaged in a parent-accessible phrase for use on kids who complain that the lawnmower is too hard to push or the stack of dirty dishes is too high to wash. Such parents were (and are) very wise to teach their children how to work hard without complaining. Passing along a work ethic to the younger generation is profitable for them, for their prospective careers, for their future families, and for generations to come.

Walking uprightly is wise. We're familiar with the notion that crime *doesn't* pay, but what about walking the "straight and narrow"? Is there anything beneficial in such behavior? According to the writer of Proverbs, it does pay to stay on that road: "The highway of the upright avoids evil; those who guard their way preserve their lives" (16:17). Life itself is our reward for walking uprightly—not only the blessing of a pulse but also an enjoyable quality of life as our conscience stands free and clear.

Walking in integrity is wise. Recently a notorious public figure lived such a duplicitous life that she had to start a file to keep track of all the lies she was telling. What a recipe for insanity! The writer of Proverbs underscored the wisdom of integrity with these words: "Whoever walks in integrity walks securely, but whoever follows perverse ways will be found out" (10:9). It's true: Honesty is still the best policy for navigating through life and the best means by which to secure peace of mind. So remember, keep on keeping it real.

Walking in humility is wise. "When pride comes, then comes disgrace; but wisdom is with the humble" (Proverbs 11:2). Some of the most gratifying moments in books and films are when arrogant, antagonistic characters finally get their comeuppance. It's even more gratifying, however, when we see good and humble characters finally cleared of misunderstanding and exalted to their proper place of honor. It's more than the stuff of fiction and fairy-tales, though. It's real life, and we are wisest when we walk humbly.

Happiness is healthy and wise. "A cheerful heart is a good medicine" (Proverbs 17:22). Sound familiar? Change a few words and you have the familiar "Laughter is the best medicine." Here's another reference to the relationship between happiness and health: "A glad heart makes a cheerful countenance, but by sorrow of heart the spirit is broken" (Proverbs 15:13). Our health encompasses our physical, emotional, mental, and spiritual well being. God wants us to take good care of ourselves by having a cheerful heart.

Seeking wisdom is wise. It may sound like a redundancy, but it's not. The quest for wisdom is wise in itself—a worthy pursuit no matter how old or young we may be. The writer of Proverbs exults: "Happy are those who find wisdom, and those who get understanding, She is more precious than jewels" (3:13, 15). Finding wisdom means that we need to look for it, and that in itself is wise.

In Christ, you are made new. "If anyone is in Christ, there is a new creation: everything old has passed away; see, everything has become new!" (2 Corinthians 5:17). In Christ, God offers us more than just a fresh start; he thoroughly remakes us from within. As part of this transformation, our me-centered motivations begin to fall away as Christ-centered love takes center stage in our hearts. Seeing life new through the clear lenses of divine love shows us the landscape as God sees it. Moreover, God helps us love people as he loves them. God wants us to know that we are truly made new.

In Christ, you are God's ambassador. "God, who reconciled us to himself through Christ, and has given us the ministry of reconciliation;...entrusting the message of reconciliation to us. So we are ambassadors for Christ" (2 Corinthians 5:18–20). As heaven's ambassadors representing Christ, we enjoy a great privilege, and we carry a solemn responsibility. As you go about your Lord's business today, you can accomplish your mission by doing his name and reputation honor by displaying his goodness, mercy, and reconciling love in the way you treat others.

In Christ, you are made for good works.
Sometimes we wonder what is our big-picture purpose. What did God make us to *do*? Is he hoping we'll change the world with a sermon, a song, or a best seller? Whether or not we possess great talent, God is not looking for us to hit grand slams to fulfill his purposes. "For we are what he has made us, created in Christ Jesus for good works, which God prepared beforehand to be our way of life" (Ephesians 2:10). Each time you choose to do what's right and good, you are living out your purpose in Christ.

In Christ, you're a citizen of heaven. "Our citizenship is in heaven, and it is from there that we are expecting a Savior, the Lord Jesus Christ" (Philippians 3:20). When we are in Christ, we receive a new citizenship—a heavenly one! That's truly amazing! (Imagine having a passport with that information on it!) One of the big changes our new citizenship brings about in our lives is a shift in our focus; temporal things don't preoccupy us as they used to, and eternal things become paramount to us. It makes perfect sense, since heaven is our true home.

In Christ, you're a child of light. The middle of the night is the perfect time for illegal activity. It affords the cover of darkness for carrying out crime. The Apostle Paul was writing about this very thing to set up this contrast: "But you, beloved, are not in darkness,... for you are all children of light and children of the day" (1 Thessalonians 5:4–5). The metaphor is familiar and clear. In Christ, we are able to live transparent lives—fully in the light, because we have the righteousness of Christ.

In Christ, you have a seat in heaven. It's disappointing when you arrive at an event you've been looking forward to, only to discover there are no good seats left. As you try to enjoy the performance or game from some far away vantage, you can't help envying those folks in the first few rows. In Christ, however, your seat in heaven is already reserved for you: "God, who is rich in mercy... made us alive together with Christ... and raised us up with him and seated us with him in the heavenly places" (Ephesians 2:4–6). And your seat *there* is sure to be astounding!

In Christ, you will conquer every adversity. The Apostle Paul is master of the pep talk to first-century Christians who were often hunted and hounded: "Who will separate us from the love of Christ? Will hardship, or distress, or persecution, or famine, or nakedness, or peril, or sword?" Paul wrote the Christians in Rome. "No, in all these things we are more than conquerors through him who loved us" (Romans 8:35, 37). You can add your own adversities to Paul's list and still own his conclusion. You, too, will overcome all these things through Christ who loves you.

Your life in Christ is like a fragrance. When we sniff the air because we've smelled something nice, we hope to discover what the fragrance is and where it's coming from. Wild roses or lilacs, an enchanting cologne, or even Sunday's simmering pot roast are aromas we like to linger over. Our lives can be like that—like a spiritual aroma that draws people to discover what we're all about: "Thanks be to God, who in Christ always leads us in triumphal procession, and through us spreads in every place the fragrance that comes from knowing him" (2 Corinthians 2:14).

You are saved by grace. People sometimes imagine that God has a great set of scales before him on which he weighs our good deeds against our bad ones—that heaven is attainable for us if our virtues finally outweigh our vices. But the reality is far different: "For by grace you have been saved through faith, and this is not your own doing; it is the gift of God—not the result of works, so that no one may boast" (Ephesians 2:8-9). Salvation can't be earned or bought because Jesus already paid for it; it's ours to be gratefully received through faith in Christ.

Christ's followers are his friends. "You are my friends if you do what I command you. I do not call you servants any longer," Jesus said, "but I have called you friends, because I have made known to you everything that I have heard from my Father" (John 15:14–15). Jesus invites his followers into a deeply committed relationship, a friendship like no other. His perfect love embraces us, giving us the courage and strength to walk in his commands. His saving grace inspires our gratitude and devotion. And his faithful companionship cheers us along our way.

You are God's temple. It may be difficult to imagine, but "Do you not know that you are God's temple and that God's Spirit dwells in you?" (1 Corinthians 3:16). God doesn't just watch your life from a distance like an umpire calling a game. When you belong to him, you receive the indwelling presence of his Spirit to accompany you, help you, and guide you. What an amazing reality! With God making his dwelling place in our hearts, he couldn't possibly be any closer to us than he is right now.

In Christ, your life bears lasting fruit. Being fruitful is about producing good things—useful and nourishing things. Jesus said, "I appointed you to go and bear fruit, fruit that will last" (John 15:16). God means for our lives to produce that which is good and lasting—that is, of eternal value. As Christ's love fills us up, the crop of his righteousness begins to ripen. Things like nurturing family members, encouraging people, and taking time to listen begin to emerge from the branches of his love within our hearts. And because Christ is our source, we can be perennially fruitful.

In Christ, you are spiritually blessed. "Blessed be the God and Father of our Lord Jesus Christ, who has blessed us in Christ with every spiritual blessing in the heavenly places" (Ephesians 1:3). *Every* spiritual blessing? That's got to be a long and awe-inspiring list. Since the blessings of salvation and God's Spirit dwelling in us are already amazing, it's hard to fathom God's generosity in opening up the floodgates of even more spiritual blessing on our lives. What is there to do but praise and thank him? Yes, "Blessed be the God and Father of our Lord Jesus Christ."

Jesus is the bread of life. Spiritual hunger is that craving we have for that "something more" beyond our physical-emotional-mental reality. When Jesus said, "I am the bread of life," he was speaking to our longing for spiritual fulfillment. Although folks may devour various pursuits, pleasures, and pastimes trying to satisfy their soul pangs, the hunger persists. Jesus knew this when he said, "Whoever comes to me will never be hungry, and whoever believes in me will never be thirsty" (John 6:35). His life is the only "food" that can fill up our famished spirits once and for all.

Jesus is the light of the world. While Christ's followers are called to be lights in a dark world, they don't have to create their own light. Their source is Christ himself. "I am the light of the world," Jesus said. "Whoever follows me will never walk in darkness but will have the light of life" (John 8:12). As you go through your days, weeks, months, and years, the Lord himself sheds his light from within you. No matter how thick the darkness may become as it presses against you, the darkness will never overcome you.

Jesus is the gate for the sheep. "I am the gate for the sheep," Jesus said. "Whoever enters by me will be saved, and will come in and go out and find pasture" (John 10:7, 9). This imagery that Jesus used to describe the way to eternal life may seem too simple, but it's not. In our quest to find our way home, we discover that God has plainly marked the way and made entering his kingdom wonderfully uncomplicated. The simple truth is that Jesus is the way to God, the way to enter his eternal kingdom of truth and love.

Jesus is the good shepherd. As children we can't wait to grow up. As adults, we often wonder why we were in such a hurry. Taking care of ourselves (and the people who rely on us) is a big job. Wouldn't it be nice to have someone taking care of us again? "I am the good shepherd. I know my own and my own know me," Jesus said. "I lay down my life for the sheep" (John 10:14–15). Jesus offers to be our protector and guardian. He even sacrificed himself to save us. Truly his care for us is like no other.

Jesus is the resurrection and the life. On the occasion of raising his friend Lazarus from the dead, Jesus said to Martha, Lazarus's sister, "I am the resurrection and the life. Those who believe in me, even though they die, will live" (John 11:25). There is no fountain of youth in this world, but there is a fountain of eternal life in Christ. Jesus, who has himself conquered death, has the power to raise us up again to everlasting life. And so, even while we enjoy life here and now, we know that, through faith in Christ, the best is yet to come!

Jesus is the way to the Father. Some of those Swiss Army knives are really something. They're like mini toolboxes. From corkscrews to tweezers, from screwdrivers to toothpicks, from blades to files—they're amazing all-in-one gadgets. "I am the way, and the truth, and the life" Jesus said. "No one comes to the Father except through me" (John 14:6). Jesus is our all-in-one Savior. We don't need a lot of different means of getting to heaven. Jesus is it—the way to God, the truth we seek, and the eternal life we hope for.

Jesus is the vine. "I am the true vine," Jesus said. "Just as the branch cannot bear fruit by itself unless it abides in the vine, neither can you unless you abide in me" (John 15:1, 4). Staying connected to our source of life is absolutely vital. It doesn't take long for a leaf to get dry and brittle after pruning it from the plant. Our spiritual life is no different. As you stay connected to Jesus through your time with him in prayer, the Scriptures, and fellowship with other believers, you remain fresh, alive, and fruitful.

The gospel is powerful. The word *gospel* means "good news." When the angelic messenger announced to the shepherds near Bethlehem that Jesus had been born, he said, "I am bringing you good news [literally, *gospel*] of great joy for all the people: to you is born this day in the city of David a Savior, who is the Messiah, the Lord" (Luke 2:10–11). The gospel is the good news of the Savior. Moreover, Paul later noted, "I am not ashamed of the gospel; it is the power of God for salvation to everyone who has faith" (Romans 1:16).

The right mindset is essential. People often talk about having the right mindset for doing something, whether it's losing weight or climbing Mount Everest. The same can be said for the Christian life—that the right mindset is essential. Paul made this point clear when he said, "Those who live according to the Spirit set their minds on the things of the Spirit" (Romans 8:5). So as we focus our thoughts on what God's Spirit is showing us, we keep moving toward our ultimate goal, for "to set the mind on the Spirit is life and peace" (verse 6).

God's Spirit helps you pray. Have you wanted to pray about something, but you just didn't know where to begin? Take comfort in this: "The Spirit helps us in our weakness; for we do not know how to pray as we ought, but that very Spirit intercedes with sighs too deep for words. And God, who searches the heart, knows what is the mind of the Spirit, because the Spirit intercedes for the saints according to the will of God" (Romans 8:26–27). Thank God! We don't always have to have the right words to reach him with our prayers.

God can make things good again. There are times when we might feel as if we've messed things up in life beyond all hope. But God is in the business of redemption—of taking messed up situations and people and restoring them. It's like those home makeover shows where they transform an unlivable space into a lovely habitation. "We know that all things work together for good for those who love God," Paul assures us, "who are called according to his purpose." (Romans 8:28). There's always hope when God is in the house.

God is your greatest ally. When it feels as if it's you versus the world, remember that God is bigger than the world, and he's on your side. "If God is for us, who is against us?" Paul asked the Christians in Rome (Romans 8:31). What Paul meant when he penned those words is not that we won't experience opposition in our life but that any opposition is no match for the power of God who's at work in us. Thanks to God, with him as our ally, no adversity can overcome us.

How to discern God's will. Perceiving the will of God is not so much about knowing whether to take a certain job or move to a certain town. It has far more to do with getting in the right mental groove: "Do not be conformed to this world, but be transformed by the renewing of your minds, so that you may discern what is the will of God—what is good and acceptable and perfect" (Romans 12:2). When our minds move from a worldly groove to a godly one, we grow in our ability to understand what pleases God.

Love is a wonderful debt. Rather than tyranniz-ing us as our Lord, Jesus graciously calls us to walk in his footsteps, requiring only that we show others the kind of love we ourselves have been shown. Our debt of love to others, therefore, is a debt of grati-tude to Christ, the one who loved us first and gave us new life. "Owe no one anything, except to love one another," said Paul, "for the one who loves another has fulfilled the law" (Romans 13:8). It's the most wonderful debt we could ever hope to owe.

The Scriptures are for your encouragement. The notion that the Bible is no longer relevant to our modern way of life is a mistaken notion: "For whatever was written in former days was written for our instruction, so that by steadfastness and by the encouragement of the scriptures we might have hope" (Romans 15:4). People's essential needs, drives, and desires have not changed, and the Bible's contents address the human condition as no other writings on earth. From the account of Creation to the story of Redemption, the pages of Scrip-ture speak eternal encouragement and hope to our hearts.

Love is essential. In the famous "Love Chapter," the Apostle Paul wrote, "If I have prophetic powers, and understand all mysteries and all knowledge, and if I have all faith, so as to remove mountains, but do not have love, I am nothing" (1 Corinthians 13:2). It's sort of like a potter working at her wheel: If the clay isn't properly centered, the potter's not going to produce anything worthwhile no matter how hard she works at it. In that light, we can see that our deeds become worthwhile only when they are centered in Christ's selfless love.

Love is patient. The first characteristic of love listed in the "Love Chapter" is patience: "Love is patient," Paul wrote (1 Corinthians 13:4). If this were the only test of love, it might just be enough. It's far harder to exercise patience among the ones we love most because we know them best. And they know us best as well. Paul, however, didn't allow for the "Familiarity breeds contempt" excuse. He knew that love can do better than that. And so it can. Therefore, remember whenever you choose the path of patience, you are walking on the high road of love.

Love is kind. Kindness is the second characteristic Paul listed in his treatise on love: "Love is kind" (1 Corinthians 13:4). Much like patience, kindness is easier to dole out to strangers than to the people whose flaws are quite familiar to us. In fact, to wrap people in kindness despite their defects is actually a divine thing to do. It's what God does for us every day of our lives—from the food we eat to the clothes we wear to the house we live in and so on, God's kindness engulfs us and reminds us of his love.

Love behaves itself. After telling us a bit about what love *is*, the Apostle Paul reminds us about what love *is not*. "Love is not envious or boastful or arrogant or rude. It does not insist on its own way; it is not irritable or resentful; it does not rejoice in wrongdoing" (1 Corinthians 13:4–6). What a flourish of no-nos! The problem is that they can be in our blind spot sometimes, and we might not recognize them in their more subtle or covert forms. A review of recent actions, words, and attitudes can let us know whether we're behaving as God wants us to behave.

Love exalts in the truth. Returning to his inventory of what love is like, Paul says that love "rejoices in the truth" (1 Corinthians 13:6). Truth comes in all shapes and sizes—from an honest witness in court to the real reason we give our boss for being late to work, from an accurate tax return to returning extra change to the cashier, from refusing a bribe to refusing to hear gossip. Love gets satisfaction from—and even delights in—the truth whenever and wherever it finds it. Moreover, love delights most of all in the one who is truth: Christ Jesus himself.

Love is tough. Anyone who's ever been married or raised children knows that love isn't for wimps. Paul wrote, "[Love] bears all things, believes all things, hopes all things, endures all things" (1 Corinthians 13:7). And by "believes all things," he didn't mean that love is naïve. Far from it! What love *believes* is that choosing to love is worthwhile even when it doesn't seem to be paying off. And even if, like the Prodigal Son, the ones we love go their own way, our love for them can remain in our prayers for their safe return to the Father.

Love is faithful. Paul finished his portrait of love with this final brushstroke: "Love never ends" (1 Corinthians 13:8). The faithful love of God is the love we're called to emulate. What does faithful love look like? Sometimes it's patient; sometimes it has to be tough. Sometimes it calls for kindness; sometimes it must speak the painful truth. But no matter what is required, it answers when called upon and waits attentively during the times of silence. If we're not sure what love should do, we need only look at Jesus, whose love is the model for Paul's portrait of true love.

Love is paramount. According to Paul, the three pillars of life in Christ are faith, hope, and love. Which was most important to Paul? He didn't hesitate to answer: "the greatest of these is love" (1 Corinthians 13:13). So when we're juggling priorities, it's good to remember that running over people in the crosswalk to get to church on time is missing the mark. And while that's an obvious exaggeration, it also brings to light the fact that Paul has come full circle in his discourse on love. Love is more important than getting stuff done—even good stuff. Love is what it's all about.

The message of love is eternal. "For this is the message you have heard from the beginning, that we should love one another" (1 John 3:11). There is a golden thread that runs throughout God's dealings with humankind. It is the strand of his undying love. In love, he weaves this thread into the hearts of his children so they, too, can carry his love to the world. And so it is that our love for one another is fashioned into the megaphone God uses to declare the eternal message of his love to all.

Love takes action. Loving words can be like icing on the cake where love is concerned, but the cake itself is made of our love in action. "Little children," said the Apostle John, "let us love, not [merely] in word or speech, but in truth and action" (1 John 3:18). Our love in action verifies who we are as Christians. Indeed, Jesus is our supreme example. In his love for us, he entered our reality on earth, walked in our shoes by experiencing temptation, lifted our burden by enduring the cross, provided eternal life by rising again, and left us his promise to return.

Love is selfless. Jesus' example has shown us what true love is like: "We know love by this, that he laid down his life for us—and we ought to lay down our lives for one another" (1 John 3:16). Each time you set aside your druthers to see to someone else's best interest, you're exercising that selfless kind of love that Jesus demonstrated. And since your motivation for self-sacrifice is out of kindness and compassion (rather than compulsion or any form of fear), the joy in giving makes each personal sacrifice well worthwhile.

Love and faith go hand in hand. "This is his commandment, that we should believe in the name of his Son Jesus Christ and love one another," wrote John. "All who obey his commandments abide in him, and he abides in them" (1 John 3:23–24). It is through faith in Christ that we're filled with his love, and it's his love flowing through us that shows our faith. That's why true love cannot operate outside of faith, and faith cannot be verified without the evidence of authentic love. Faith and love: The two go hand in hand.

The kingdom of God is the greatest blessing. "Among those born of women no one is greater than John [the Baptist]," Jesus said, "yet the least in the kingdom of God is greater than he" (Luke 7:28). With these puzzling words, Jesus challenged his listeners to discover what he was conveying, knowing that if they did, they'd realize what is the greatest blessing ever. While John the Baptist had the distinction of preparing the way for Christ, sadly John died before seeing Jesus open the way into God's kingdom. In that sense, those of us who receive salvation in this life are exceedingly blessed.

The kingdom of God is good news. Jesus "went on through cities and villages, proclaiming and bringing the good news of the kingdom of God" (Luke 8:1). To the people of his day, Jesus announced the good news this way: "The kingdom of heaven is near." And it was *near* since Jesus was about to usher it in through his death and resurrection. Today, because Jesus accomplished what he came to do, the good news we have is this: "The kingdom of heaven is *here*." We can enter God's kingdom right now through Jesus Christ, and that's really good news!

The kingdom of heaven reaches out to everyone. "Again," Jesus said, "the kingdom of heaven is like a net that was thrown into the sea and caught fish of every kind" (Matthew 13:47). The message of salvation through Christ has gone out into the world, even to remote tribes in distant lands. In fact, as you read this, Bible societies are busy translating the Scriptures into the native languages of various cultures so that they can read God's Word for themselves in their own tongue. God wants people everywhere to be saved and enter into his kingdom of light and life.

The kingdom of heaven flourishes. "The kingdom of heaven is like a mustard seed," Jesus said. "It is the smallest of all the seeds, but when it has grown it...becomes a tree, so that the birds...make nests in its branches" (Matthew 13:31–32). God's kingdom grows in more ways than one. It has, of course, spread throughout the world. But also, since the good news of God's kingdom is that salvation is through faith in Christ, it takes root in our hearts. It then branches out from our lives in various expressions of God's love and mercy to those around us.

The kingdom of heaven is worth everything. "The kingdom of heaven is like a merchant in search of fine pearls," Jesus said. "On finding one pearl of great value, he went and sold all that he had and bought it" (Matthew 13:45–46). It's interesting what things we value. Each person is different in what he or she values. Many people would put family and friends at the top of their list, with health and wealth not far behind. But what about eternal life in God's heavenly kingdom? Jesus said it's worth absolutely everything to acquire it.

The kingdom of heaven calls for childlike faith. "Truly I tell you," Jesus said, "unless you change and become like children, you will never enter the kingdom of heaven" (Matthew 18:3). Jesus isn't calling us to be *childish people,* but to have *childlike faith.* Entering God's kingdom means taking him at his word, just as a child trusts a good and loving parent. And while we won't always understand God's ways as he works in our lives, we can be sure he's always looking out for our best interest.

The kingdom of God is good news. Jesus "went on through cities and villages, proclaiming and bringing the good news of the kingdom of God" (Luke 8:1). To the people of his day, Jesus announced the good news this way: "The kingdom of heaven is near." And it was *near* because Jesus was about to usher it in through his death and resurrection. Today, because Jesus accomplished what he came to do, the good news we have is this: "The kingdom of heaven is *here.*" We can enter God's kingdom right now through Christ, and that's really good news!

The kingdom of God welcomes all who believe. "People will come from east and west, from north and south, and will eat in the kingdom of God" (Luke 13:29). It's an insightful picture of wonderful diversity—a feast of various peoples celebrating around God's banquet table! The kingdom of God is not exclusive to any one race or nationality; it's open to all who will trust in Christ for salvation. And because Jesus has opened the kingdom of heaven to us, God welcomes everyone who wishes to receive his gifts of love, mercy, grace, and eternal life.

God's kingdom is spiritual. "The kingdom of God is not coming with things that can be observed," Jesus said. "Nor will they say, 'Look, here it is!' or 'There it is!' For, in fact, the kingdom of God is among you" (Luke 17:20–21). Jesus himself was the one who was among his listeners, revealing God's kingdom as he taught, healed, and performed all sorts of miracles. After his resurrection, it became clear that he hadn't come to establish or take over an earthly kingdom; instead, he came to open the heavenly kingdom to all who would put their trust in him.

The spiritual life is born through Christ.
"Very truly, I tell you," Jesus said, "no one can see the kingdom of God without being born from above" (John 3:3). We know that physical birth endows us with physical life, but comprehending how the spiritual life is born might seem difficult to grasp. Jesus made it clear, however, that we need a spiritual birth to enter his kingdom. So how is this spiritual birth accomplished? It's through Christ—that is, receiving his saving grace by faith—that we come to life spiritually. It's really quite simple and yet wholly essential for eternal life.

The essence of God's kingdom is peace and joy. "The kingdom of God is not food and drink but righteousness and peace and joy in the Holy Spirit" (Romans 14:17). The saying "Essence is more important than form" is especially true of the spiritual life. We can try to look pious by what we wear, how we pray aloud, what we include in or exclude from our diet, and so on, but it's only when we "walk the walk" with a heart tuned to God's Spirit that we avoid being mere posers. Indeed, peace and joy mark the heart—the essence—of every true believer.

God never loses track of you. "I've got my eye on you," an authority figure warns as he tries to intimidate a delinquent who's skating on thin ice. By contrast, when *God* says, "I've got my eye on you," he's not threatening; he's making a fantastic promise—a powerful assurance of his help and guidance. God wants you to know: "I will instruct you and teach you the way you should go; I will counsel you with my eye upon you" (Psalm 32:8). If you feel forgotten by God, you aren't; God hasn't lost track of you, and he never will.

God enables us to remain faithful. "May your spirit and soul and body be kept sound and blameless at the coming of our Lord Jesus Christ. The one who calls you is faithful, and he will do this" (1 Thessalonians 5:23–24). When we hear words like "blameless," we get uneasy. How can we be kept *blameless* in this life? Well, if it were up to us, we'd fall far short. But it is the one who has called us to be blameless that accomplishes this in us, faithfully working in our lives and preparing us for the day of his promised return.

Praising God keeps you positive. Let's face it, we don't always *feel* like praising God. Pain, frustration, sorrow, and disappointment are all a part of living in a fallen world. But if during difficult times, we can muster an offering of praise for what's still right in the world, we begin to see our situation from a place above it, rather than from beneath. Therefore, "Let us continually offer a sacrifice of praise to God, that is, the fruit of lips that confess his name" (Hebrews 13:15). So even if your praise must begin through gritted teeth, lift it up anyway.

God works in mysterious ways. Of course, that isn't an actual Bible verse, but the principle is definitely in the Scriptures. The writer of Ecclesiastes 11:5 says, "Just as you do not know how the breath comes to the bones in the mother's womb, so you do not know the work of God, who makes everything." What are we to make of God's mysterious ways? Well, perhaps it's as simple as realizing that the best thing we can do sometimes is stop trying to figure out what God's doing and just quietly trust that he's doing what's best for us.

Your life is in God's hands. "The Lord will keep you from all evil," wrote the psalmist. "He will keep your life. The Lord will keep your going out and your coming in from this time on and forevermore" (Psalm 121:7–8). In all your comings and goings, God has kept you alive to this day. That's a pretty amazing thing when you consider how fragile the human body is and how many hazards there are all around us. So each new day God grants us, let's return thanks by living for him.

God loves cheerful giving. When we give to others, do we do it joyfully, knowing that all we have God has given to us. "Each of you must give as you have made up your mind," said Paul, "not reluctantly or under compulsion, for God loves a cheerful giver" (2 Corinthians 9:7). A good portion of our day can end up being spent giving to others—especially if we're filling a caretaking role. While it's often easier to cheerfully write a check for a good cause than it is to go another round of caring for people's needs, even this giving can be done with a glad heart as we offer each act of service as a gift of love to God.

God cares for the vulnerable. While God doesn't play favorites, he does notice those among us who are at a social disadvantage. "The Lord," said the writer of Deuteronomy, "executes justice for the orphan and the widow, and ... loves the strangers, providing them food and clothing" (Deuteronomy 10:17–18). God sees those who suffer socially and economically; he cares about them and looks after them, offering his own provision and protection to meet their needs. And as God's children, we're called to reach out with God's love to each of them.

God loves justice. "The Lord loves justice," said the psalmist. "He will not forsake his faithful ones" (Psalm 37:28). Justice can seem like a harsh, steely concept, but it's really a part of God's good character. God loves what is right and true, and his justice is all about that. While it sometimes may seem to us as though injustice is prevailing in this world, God sees and knows the truth, and he will bring his own justice to bear on the unjust. We may not see it right now, but it's coming. Moreover, God will not forsake his people.

God values righteousness. Although God loves everyone, the choices we make about how we will live have a bearing on our relationship with him. "The Lord is righteous; he loves righteous deeds; the upright shall behold his face" (Psalm 11:7). We seek to walk in ways that please God because we're grateful to him and love him. He honors us for that attitude, and the relationship we develop with him as we walk in his ways draws us ever nearer to him.

God loves those who stand up for what's right. It can be intimidating to stand up for what we know to be right and good and true—especially when we're the only one standing. But God supports those who choose his ways and who refuse to cave in to the pressure to do what would be evil in God's sight. "The Lord loves those who hate evil; he guards the lives of his faithful; he rescues them from the hand of the wicked" (Psalm 97:10). So take courage!

God's love is evident all around you. If you were a detective looking for clues about God's love, you'd be able to gather lots of evidence in a short time just by contemplating this world he has made: "The earth is full of the steadfast love of the Lord" (Psalm 33:5). Taking a moment each day to marvel at God's works is not only an affirmation of the reality of his love for us but also a meaningful act of worship as we delight in him—the one who has so plainly inscribed his love everywhere.

God the Father loves his Son. The profound love God has for his Son gives us confidence in his love for us. "The Father loves the Son and has placed all things in his hands," said the Apostle John. "Whoever believes in the Son has eternal life" (John 3:35–36). The Son took on the work of securing our salvation, while the Father relinquished his dear Son for that painful work. For both Father and Son, it was the supreme sacrifice because of their perfect love for us. And it's that love that calls us to believe.

God loves everyone. You mean *everyone*? Even _____? No matter whose name we place in that blank, the answer is yes. God extends his love to us, not based on our deserving it, but because he is good and full of mercy. His desire is to spend the rest of eternity with us: "For God so loved the world that he gave his only Son, so that everyone who believes in him may not perish but may have eternal life" (John 3:16). But he leaves the choice up to us.

God loves those who love his Son. "The Father himself loves you," Jesus said, "because you have loved me and have believed that I came from God" (John 16:27). All this talk about God's love! Is that all God has to tell us? Well, it may not be all, but it *is* the heart of his eternal message. God loves us! Can you think of a more wonderful theme? And our love for the Son stirs the Father's love for us as well.

God's love initiated a relationship with us. "In this is love, not that we loved God but that he loved us and sent his Son to be the atoning sacrifice for our sins," said John. "We love because he first loved us" (1 John 4:10, 19). So often in our relationships we have a "you first" attitude when it comes to risking or being vulnerable. We might wait for the other person to apologize first or say I love you first. Not God. He was willing to risk everything to offer us his love. So he loves first.

We can praise God for his love. As God's children, we should let God know how thankful we are to him for his love. To get there, we can ask ourselves, "What might my life look like right now if God's love hadn't found me?" Then with thankful hearts, we can praise our Father in heaven: "To him who loves us and freed us from our sins by his blood, . . . to him be glory and dominion forever and ever" (Revelation 1:5-6). God wants us to know that we can praise him freely and openly for his love for us.

Obedience demonstrates love for God. Actions speak louder than words, right? It's not that words aren't important, of course. (Many of us need to hear the loving words along with the actions.) But it's our actions that ultimately prove our love for God. "They who have my commandments and keep them," said Jesus, "are those who love me" (John 14:21). So what are our actions saying about our love for God? Each act of obedience is an "I love you" that makes our words of love and devotion ring true in God's ear.

God calls us to imitate his love. As God's children, we're called to walk in his footsteps: "Therefore be imitators of God, as beloved children, and live in love, as Christ loved us and gave himself up for us, a fragrant offering and sacrifice to God" (Ephesians 5:1–2). When it comes to loving others sacrificially, we've got some big shoes to fill. God, however, hasn't left us alone to try walking in them; his Spirit helps us love as Christ loves.

God ordained times and seasons. We may move our clocks ahead or back to take advantage of daylight hours, but we can never change the times or the seasons set by divine decree: "Yours is the day, yours also the night; you established the luminaries and the sun. You have fixed all the bounds of the earth;

you made summer and winter" (Psalm 74:16–17). We watch days come and go with their sunrises and sunsets. We note the moon's changing phases. We anticipate each new season. And we acknowledge the greatness of God who made them all.

God sustains the earth. The Lord God is the Creator of all good things, and he has assigned us stewardship responsibilities on earth—to care for its creatures and manage its resources—but God himself sustains the earth's existence and the life of each plant and animal. As grave concerns over the earth's future swirl around us, we can find peace of mind in God's promise to Noah after the great flood: "As long as the earth endures, seedtime and harvest, cold and heat, summer and winter, day and night, shall not cease" (Genesis 8:22). If we seek to be good stewards here, we can trust God with our future.

God knows all the mysteries of nature. "Have you entered the storehouses of the snow, or have you seen the storehouses of the hail?" God asked

Job. "What is the way to the place where the light is distributed, or where the east wind is scattered upon the earth?" (Job 38:22, 24). We stand mutely with Job, not able to fathom the vast knowledge and wisdom of God. And so, if he knows the mysteries of nature, he certainly knows me through and through.

God reveals the constellations. We watch the constellations move across the sky in their seasons, but we can only watch: "Can you bind the chains of the Pleiades, or loose the cords of Orion?" God asked Job. "Can you . . . guide the Bear with its children?" (Job 38:31–32). No, we can't. God alone can send them sprawling across the night sky at their proper time. As we recognize his sovereign power in the universe, our trust in him becomes strong and unshakable.

God gave animals their unique traits. Who doesn't enjoy a delightful encounter with one of God's creatures? Whether it's an eagle soaring overhead or a chipmunk begging for a handout, we're fascinated by his animal kingdom. He uniquely fashioned each species: "Can you hunt the prey for the lion?" God asked Job. "Who has let the wild ass go free?...Do you give the horse its might?...Is it by your wisdom that the hawk soars?" (Job 38:39; 39:5, 19, 26). Truly we are mesmerized when we see the creative display of God's wisdom in all he has made.

God provides for all the creatures he has made. God has been providing for his creation since he first spoke it into existence and fashioned humankind from the dust. "The eyes of all look to you, and you give them their food in due season," the psalmist said to God. "You open your hand, satisfying the desire of every living thing" (Psalm 145:15–16). For millennia, yearly harvests have brought sustenance from his hand. It's something that reveals God's faithful love; he feeds us when we think of him and thank him, and even when we don't.

God directs times, seasons, and events. "For everything there is a season, and a time for every matter under heaven" (Ecclesiastes 3:1). That God sees and is able to orchestrate the times and seasons of nature, as well as the events of our lives, reminds us that he is both omniscient (all knowing) and omnipotent (all powerful).

You can entrust the times and seasons of your life to God. People sometimes stress out if life doesn't go as they'd hoped or planned. For example, they may think they should be married by a certain age or have a certain amount of money in the bank or be retired by a certain time in life. That our goals and agendas often go unmet underscores the fact that much in life is beyond our control. That's why the psalmist declared, "I trust in you, O Lord...My times are in your hand" (Psalm 31:14–15).

God invites everyone to be saved. Have you ever felt left out or rejected? From being the last one picked for dodgeball to having someone dear to you walk away, all rejection is painful. In his love for us, Jesus endured rejection, too, so our names could be included on his gracious invitation to live with him in heaven: "God our Savior," Paul said, "desires everyone to be saved and to come to the knowledge of the truth" (1 Timothy 2:3–4). The Savior requests the pleasure of your company in eternity with him. His invitation awaits your RSVP.

God desires truthfulness. "You desire truth in the inward being; therefore teach me wisdom in my secret heart" (Psalm 51:6). King David wrote these words after he was forced to come to terms with a horrible lapse in his integrity. Knowing that fellowship with God requires truthfulness and authenticity, David asked God to restore him to being a man whose heart was set on truth. David knew that fake piety is useless in approaching God but that honest penitence is the perfect starting place for growing in genuine relationship with him.

Proper respect pleases God. "His delight is not in the strength of the horse, nor his pleasure in the speed of a runner; but the Lord takes pleasure in those who fear him, in those who hope in his steadfast love" (Psalm 147:10–11). While fame and fortune may wow people, God's value system is more about what's inside us than about what we can accomplish. The kinds of things that make God's heart glad have to do with our trust in him, how we relate to him, and how we show our love in return.

Prayers from an upright heart please God. "The sacrifice of the wicked is an abomination to the Lord, but the prayer of the upright is his delight" (Proverbs 15:8). Just as we are thrilled with the smallest act of tenderness from our loved ones, so God loves even our quietest acts of trust—our prayers. God sees past what we bring in our hands to the contents of our hearts. He cherishes the petitions, requests, and praises of his beloved children, delighting in them at all times.

God is worth "boasting" about. "Do not let the wise boast in their wisdom, ... the mighty boast in their might, ... the wealthy boast in their wealth,"

declared the Lord, "but let those who boast boast in this, that they understand and know me" (Jeremiah 9:23–24). It might seem strange to think of "boasting" about knowing God, but the "boasting" God is talking about has to do with our praises of him as we delight in his steadfast love and righteousness.

Walking humbly with God pleases him. "He has told you, O mortal, what is good," said the prophet Micah, "and what does the Lord require of you but to do justice, and to love kindness, and to walk humbly with your God?" (Micah 6:8). So, what does it look like to walk humbly with God? For each person, the particulars are quite different, but the essence is always the same. Remain humble and walk in a manner that pleases the Lord.

God delights in showing mercy. God's mercy surpasses even his righteous anger. "Who is a God like you, pardoning iniquity and passing over the transgression . . . ?" asked Micah. "He does not retain his anger forever, because he delights in showing clemency" (Micah 7:18). In fact, the moment we sincerely seek his forgiveness, his mercy is poised to pardon us and set us on the right path again. Even more amazing is that God extends this undeserved kindness to us, not with irritation, but with delight.

God made the heavens and the earth. "In six days the Lord made heaven and earth, the sea, and all that is in them" (Exodus 20:11). For those who believe God is the Creator, there is great comfort in knowing that such a powerful and creative God also cares deeply for what he has made. As you remember your loving Creator today, delight in this simple benediction: "May you be blessed by the Lord, who made heaven and earth" (Psalm 115:15).

God presides over heaven and earth. There's nothing that escapes God's notice. Everything that transpires in heaven and on earth is in his view. "The Lord your God is indeed God in heaven above and on earth below" (Joshua 2:11). While God permits people to choose their path in life, no human plan will ever prevail against God's purposes. He is God, and he presides with wisdom over all things.

God's dwelling is in heaven. God is everywhere, and yet his throne is beyond the universe in a place the Scriptures call "heaven." "The Lord is in his holy temple; the Lord's throne is in heaven. His eyes behold...humankind" (Psalm 11:4). God walked the earth in the person of Jesus, who now rules with his Father in heaven. Meanwhile, his Spirit dwells in us. Yes, God is in heaven, and yet he is also with us.

God affirmed his Son from heaven. "When Jesus also had been baptized...a voice came from heaven, 'You are my Son, the Beloved; with you I am well pleased'" (Luke 3:21–22). Not long after his baptism, Jesus chose his disciples and often reminded them that he had come to do the will of his Father in heaven. How would they know he was on track? Well, God the Father publicly said so. By speaking this way, the Father not only affirmed his Son but also encouraged Jesus' followers to trust in him.

Heaven rejoices over penitent people. "I tell you," Jesus said, "there will be more joy in heaven over one sinner who repents than over ninety-nine righteous persons who need no repentance" (Luke 15:7). It's not that God doesn't value those who are already walking with him; it's that the ones who are lost deeply concern him. We love our children, and we're grateful if they grow up avoiding harmful addictions, destructive behaviors, and damaging relationships. But if they do get into trouble, our hearts are grieved. Yet, if they return to God, we're overjoyed . . . and so is heaven.

Jesus ascended into heaven. The Scriptures tell us that Jesus appeared publicly a number of times after his resurrection. Then, after leaving final instructions to his disciples to spread the good news of salvation to the world, he ascended into heaven. "The Lord Jesus, after he had spoken to them, was taken up into heaven and sat down at the right hand of God" (Mark 16:19). It is in heaven that Jesus awaits the Father's signal to return to earth in glory for those who belong to him.

Jesus promised to return from heaven. When Jesus ascended into heaven, he was taken up in the clouds. The Scriptures tell us that he will return the same way. "You will see the Son of Man seated at the right hand of Power," Jesus said, "and coming on the clouds of heaven" (Matthew 26:64). It is such a wondrous event that his followers eagerly anticipate it.

Jesus sent the Holy Spirit from heaven. Jesus promised that he would send his Spirit to comfort, help, and teach his followers after his ascension into heaven. After Jesus' departure, as the first Christians prayed together in an upstairs room, a momentous event occurred. "Suddenly from heaven there came a sound like the rush of a violent wind.... All of them were filled with the Holy Spirit" (Acts 2:2, 4). This event truly fulfilled Jesus' promise.

God's Word is eternal. The words we speak often are forgotten. At times, we may even forget promises we've made! God, however, remembers every word he's spoken, and he stands by his promises. When we take hold of his Word, we can be certain he will be faithful to it. "Heaven and earth will pass away," Jesus said, "but my words will not pass away" (Mark 13:31).

God's Word always accomplishes its purpose. In what way is God's Word like the rain and snow? "As the rain and the snow come down from heaven, and do not return there until they have watered the earth, making it bring forth and sprout, giving seed to the sower and bread to the eater, so shall my word be" (Isaiah 55:10–11). Whether it's to correct, teach, warn, encourage, or help us in some way, the Word of God always succeeds.

God's Word is reliable. Some travelers to remote areas of the world tell hair-raising stories about crossing steep ravines over rickety footbridges. Some boards were missing, and others were weak. They had to pick their way along and hope for the best. Some people feel as if God's Word is like that—that they have to pick what parts of Scripture are reliable. But in reality, God's Word is always solid ground. "Every word of God proves true; he is a shield to those who take refuge in him" (Proverbs 30:5).

❋

God's Word is like seed. The Bible says our hearts are like soil, and God's Word is like seed planted there. "As for that [seed planted] in the good soil," said Jesus, the good soil "are the ones who, when they hear the word, hold it fast in an honest and good heart, and bear fruit with patient endurance" (Luke 8:15). The soil of a ready heart is one that, after receiving God's Word, never lets go of it.

❋

Jesus is God's Word in the flesh. Besides God's written Word, God has also given us his living Word—Jesus. "In the beginning was the Word, and the Word was with God, and the Word was God" (John 1:1). In Jesus' miracles, we see God's power over nature. In Jesus' teaching, we see God's wisdom. In Jesus' atoning death, we see God's mercy. And in Jesus' resurrection, we see God's triumph over death. In Jesus, we clearly see the living God.

God's Word gets to the heart of a matter. To subject our hearts to the Word of God is, spiritually speaking, like going under the surgeon's scalpel. "The word of God is living and active, sharper than any two-edged sword...; it is able to judge the thoughts and intentions of the heart" (Hebrews 4:12). As we begin to apply the Bible's instruction to our lives, some attitudes, thoughts, and actions will be singled out for removal: That resentment, that gossip, that pride—they all have to go. But after the surgery, what a relief! It's like having a fresh start!

God created the universe by his Word. What if suddenly we could all speak and have our words come to pass? We'd quickly learn the meaning of chaos. Fortunately when God spoke the universe into existence, he could pause after each phase of his work and call it good. "By faith we understand that the worlds were prepared by the word of God, so that what is seen was made from things that are not visible" (Hebrews 11:3). His mere words, though invisible, brought forth this visible world. We can't prove it by science, but, by faith, we believe it's true.

God's Word safeguards us. Why do we need God's Word? "I treasure your word in my heart," said the psalmist, "so that I may not sin against you" (Psalm 119:11). The straight and narrow way is impossible to keep without the ongoing support of Scripture. It's easy to understand why: Worldly influences can wear us down; our own fickle moods can play tricks on us; and peer pressure can get the better of us. But by continually holding up the truth of God's Word against our human perceptions, we gain the perspective and strength we need to stay on the righteous course God has plotted for us.

God helps us understand his Word. "Open my eyes," the psalmist said to God, "so that I may behold wondrous things out of your law" (Psalm 119:18). It's common to hear Christians exclaim, "Before I was a Christian, the Bible made no sense to me. Now I understand!" That's what the psalmist was talking about—grasping the truth of the Scriptures as God's Spirit reveals God's wisdom to us. It's exciting when our eyes are opened, and we see the "wondrous things" God wants us to know in his Word.

God's Word is a good counselor. Sound advice is always consistent with the Word of God. That being said, how do we know what God's Word says? Well, we need to read it, listen to it, and study it. It takes time, but little by little with consistent exposure, we gain an understanding of what God has to say to us. "Your decrees are my delight," said the psalmist, "they are my counselors" (Psalm 119:24). It truly is the best resource for navigating life.

God's Word is encouraging. The psalms are a great resource for encouragement. "My soul melts away for sorrow," said the psalmist. "Strengthen me according to your word" (Psalm 119:28). The psalms reveal the raw emotions of people who were honest about their difficulties. They include poet-warriors, sage-kings, and songwriter clergy—an assortment of humanity whose joys and sorrows are chronicled, in part, for our comfort and encouragement. Whether you're singing the blues or walking on air, God wants you to know that there is a psalm to meet you where you are—to comfort your hurting heart or to fill your mouth with thanksgiving.

God's Word brings freedom. "I shall walk at liberty," said the psalmist, "for I have sought your precepts" (Psalm 119:45). There's freedom in doing things God's way. It's the freedom of a clear conscience, the freedom of nothing to hide, and the freedom of having no sin standing in the way of our fellowship with God. And with freedom come the blessings of joy and peace as well.

God's Word brings hope. When life is sinking to the depths, hope is buoyant. The Word of God is a lifeline of hope when despair comes knocking—and it's not just the kind of hope that crosses its fingers. It's complete confidence, knowing that God always keeps his Word. "Remember your word to your servant, in which you have made me hope," said the psalmist. "This is my comfort in my distress, that your promise gives me life" (Psalm 119:49–50).

God's Word is a teacher. "The unfolding of your words gives light," said the psalmist. "It imparts understanding to the simple" (Psalm 119:130). The psalmist knew that compared to the Lord God, everyone who's ever lived, including Solomon, Einstein, and the latest Jeopardy champ, are far from being as wise as God. For all the smarts we may have, without God's wisdom guiding us, we're stuck in preschool (spiritually speaking). But God is more than willing to teach us; he's even provided us with an amazing curriculum: his written Word.

God's Word is immovable. When God speaks, it's set in stone. "The Lord exists forever; your word is firmly fixed in heaven," said the psalmist. "Your faithfulness endures to all generations; you have established the earth, and it stands fast" (Psalm 119:89–90). When God says we're forgiven, we're forgiven. When he says he loves us, he loves us. When he says he's coming back for us, we can count on it. You have his word on it.

God rewards steadfast hearts. Great things will surely come to those who remain faithful to God.

"Blessed is anyone who endures temptation. Such a one has stood the test and will receive the crown of life that the Lord has promised to those who love him" (James 1:12). That's why when frustration or discouragement tempt us to compromise or give up, we mustn't give in! Rather, we need to remember that we've got a blessing—a crown of life—waiting for us when we arrive safely home.

God does not tempt. God wants us to know that "No one, when tempted, should say, 'I am being tempted by God'; for God cannot be tempted by evil and he himself tempts no one" (James 1:13). The devil tempted the first couple in the Garden of Eden, and he's been at it ever since. And because God loves righteousness and hates wickedness, he would never tempt us. Therefore, when we're being tempted, don't think God is luring us to do evil. He's not!

All good gifts come from God. Everything that's truly good originates from our heavenly Father. Indeed, "every generous act of giving, with every perfect gift, is from above, coming down from the Father of lights, with whom there is no variation or shadow due to change" (James 1:17). God doesn't change, and neither do his kind intentions toward us, which we see in every good gift he gives us.

God blesses those who act on his Word. "Those who look into the perfect law, the law of liberty, and persevere, being not hearers who forget but doers who act—they will be blessed in their doing" (James 1:25). James compared reading God's Word to using a mirror. If we look into a mirror and see dirt smudges on our face, we wash up. Similarly, when we hold our lives up to God's Word, we can see what needs to change. So James tells us to look at what God's Word has revealed and take action.

Living to please God brings lasting fulfillment. God is the best gift giver. To the ones who draw near to him, who enjoy walking with him, and who want to please him, he gives what will benefit them most and yet cannot be taken away. "To the one who pleases him God gives wisdom and knowledge and joy" (Ecclesiastes 2:26). God gives gifts of lasting fulfillment to those whose hearts seek to please him.

Only God can genuinely change you. In our search for spiritual wholeness, a no-half-measures principle applies. How is that? First, we must look *only* to God, and second, we must seek him *wholeheartedly*. "Heal me, O Lord, and I shall be healed," said the prophet Jeremiah. "Save me, and I shall be saved; for you are my praise" (Jeremiah 17:14). Truly, there's no salvation and no healing outside of the Lord! Moreover, God wants us to know that only those who seek him wholeheartedly will find him.

Wisdom from God is pure. God's wisdom doesn't say one thing and do another. Nor does it fawn over the wealthy and beautiful people while ignoring "ordinary" folks in its circles. "The wisdom from above is first pure, then peaceable, gentle, willing to yield, full of mercy and good fruits, without a trace of partiality or hypocrisy" (James 3:17). It seeks peace, chooses mercy over retribution, and enjoys showing kindness. These are the hallmarks of God's wisdom at work in the lives of his people.

God wants you to draw near. God wants to be close to us. "Draw near to God, and he will draw near to you" (James 4:8). Isn't that an astonishing reality? He didn't just start the earth a-spinning and then leave us to fend for ourselves. No, God invites us to draw near to him, and when we demonstrate our desire for relationship with him by responding to that invitation, he responds by drawing near to us.

Prayer is powerful. Do you ever wonder if your prayers do any good? Well, James says that prayers are "powerful and effective" when they come from those walking in right relationship with God: "The prayer of the righteous is powerful and effective" (James 5:16). That means that results are on the way.

Sometimes we see those results immediately, but not always, and not always in the form we expect, but God brings his wisdom to bear on our requests and works in a way and in the timing that's best for us.

You can approach God boldly. Not just anyone is permitted to walk into the Oval Office and speak with the President of the United States. An appointment must be made—unless, of course, you're one of his own children. Similarly, God's children have privileges of full access to their Father's presence, an open door to come in without appointment or apology. "Let us therefore approach the throne of grace with boldness, so that we may receive mercy and find grace to help in time of need" (Hebrews 4:16). The Lord always welcomes us.

Our hope is in God's promises. When we tell others about our faith in Christ, we point to God's promises: his promise to forgive us if we confess our sin; his promise to save us if we'll trust in Christ; his promise to give us eternal life; his promise to never leave us; and his promise to return. "Let us hold fast to the confession of our hope without wavering, for he who has promised is faithful" (Hebrews 10:23). God wants us to know that if our hope is firmly set on his promises, he will fulfill them.

Encouragement is found in fellowship. Going to church isn't a requirement for being a Christian, but Christians *do* need each other. "Let us consider how to provoke one another to love and good deeds, not neglecting to meet together, ... but encouraging one another" (Hebrews 10:24–25). Worshiping together is one of many ways to stay connected. Other ways include volunteering to be part of a ministry team; praying together; and joining a Bible study group. Whatever you do, just remember that God wants you to stay connected.

Thanksgiving is a form of worship. Sometimes we think of worship in terms of what transpires in a church service, but worship includes every act of devotion to God, including every time we thank him for something—thanks at mealtime, thanks for a sunset, thanks for health, thanks for a warm shower, and so on. "Since we are receiving a kingdom that cannot be shaken, let us give thanks, by which we offer to God an acceptable worship with reverence and awe" (Hebrews 12:28). Whatever thanks is in your heart, when you offer it up to God, it's a true form of worship.

Good spiritual leaders are worth following.
The best spiritual leaders speak with their lives as well as with their words. "Remember your leaders, those who spoke the word of God to you; consider the outcome of their way of life, and imitate their faith" (Hebrews 13:7). When we find a leader whose life lines up with their message, we can happily follow their example and confidently encourage others to do the same. Faithful leaders are gifts from God, and whenever we find them, we should show our gratitude to God for them by encouraging them in their work.

Christ offers ultimate healing. During his time on earth, Jesus demonstrated his divine power to heal disability, sickness, and disease. But this was just a foretaste of what he was yet to do once his work on the cross was complete. "Surely he has borne our infirmities and carried our diseases," said the prophet Isaiah. "... upon him was the punishment that made us whole, and by his bruises we are healed" (Isaiah 53:4–5). Now, thanks to Jesus, we can experience the most profound aspect of his healing ministry: his power to heal our broken relationship with God and restore our spiritual well being.

Christ has set you free. Trying to follow all the rules perfectly is an exercise in futility: Did I follow every one correctly? Did I miss one? What if I *did* miss one? Jesus came to change that way of thinking by changing how we live in relationship to God by granting us a new heart. Under this new arrangement, secured by Christ's atonement on the cross, we no longer live under the fearful letter of the law, but freely as the Spirit leads us in true righteousness. "For freedom Christ has set us free" (Galatians 5:1).

Jesus is unwavering. It's said that the shifting times, people, and places of this world are like sinking sand! They are never solid, always changing under our feet, and often disappointing us. But Jesus Christ is just the opposite of that: He is reliable, faithful, and true. Moreover, "Jesus Christ is the same yesterday and today and forever" (Hebrews 13:8). He never changes, and we can depend on his steadfast love to see us through.

Doing good to people pleases God. As we receive good things from God's hand, we will always have opportunities to share his gifts with others. "Do not neglect to do good and to share what you have, for such sacrifices are pleasing to God" (Hebrews 13:16). The Lord smiles on our benevolence, as we find ways to bless not only those around us but also those in places more distant.

Peace is an ongoing goal. While being in a peaceful place makes life seem effortless, getting to that place is not always easy. It often takes a concerted effort to reach a peaceful outcome. Meanwhile, we should "pursue peace with everyone" (Hebrews 12:14). To get there, honorable compromises are sometimes required or a heart-felt apology might be in order. Moreover, a listening ear, as well as an understanding heart, is indispensable in the pursuit of lasting peace. Situations will always arise to challenge godly peace, but if we make peace our goal, God will help us in our quest and show us how to achieve it.

God is the source of true peace. We could write a million peace treaties and establish diplomatic relations with every nation, but without God's intervention, lasting peace will always elude us, for God himself is the source of true peace. He alone can grant us the peace we seek. "The Lord bless you and keep you; the Lord make his face to shine upon you, and be gracious to you;...and give you peace" (Numbers 6:24–26). It's wonderful to know that when he fully ushers in his kingdom, we'll enjoy everlasting peace.

God grants peaceful sleep. Remaining confident that the Lord God has everything under control is a peaceful way to go about life. As you trust God for what lies ahead, you can even enjoy peaceful sleep, even if by all appearances things look chaotic and scary: "I will both lie down and sleep in peace," said the psalmist. "For you alone, O Lord, make me lie down in safety" (Psalm 4:8). It's not a matter of blocking out reality to live in a la-la land. Rather, it's knowing that, despite one's troubles, God is taking good care of us.

Choosing what is good brings peace. Part of what brings peace into our circumstances is making good choices—that is, choosing what's morally right and refusing what's morally wrong. The psalmist hit on the direct correlation between peace and right living when he wrote, "Depart from evil, and do good; seek peace, and pursue it" (Psalm 34:14). As we make right choices, we create an environment of peace for ourselves and for those around us. Of course, making good choices may sometimes provoke temporary resistance or conflict, but the ultimate outcome is authentic peace.

God encourages his people with peace. Sometimes we just need to hear God speaking peace to us, soothing and reminding us of his deep love for us. At times we might hear his voice through a Bible passage or maybe through someone else's encouragement or even in the sense we have of his peaceful presence. "Let me hear what God the Lord will speak," said the psalmist, "for he will speak peace to his people, to his faithful, to those who turn to him in their hearts" (Psalm 85:8). In many gentle ways, our heavenly Father speaks peace to us, his children.

Following God's ways brings peace. Have you ever noticed that when you're in the presence of someone who has God's peace, there's a wonderful stillness that seems to accompany them? Their demeanor is pleasant, their conversation is calming, and their serenity soothes away people's tensions and frustrations. What is it about them? God's Word tells us that those who walk in God's ways enjoy the blessings of an unshakable peace: "Great peace have those who love your law," said the psalmist. "Nothing can make them stumble" (Psalm 119:165).

Walking in wisdom is a peaceful way of life.
Wise people reap many benefits along their chosen
path, including the peace that wisdom brings.
"[Wisdom's] ways are ways of pleasantness," the
author of Proverbs 3:17 tells us, "and all her paths
are peace." But, of course, a peaceful path doesn't
mean a boring path. There is plenty of adventure
to be had on the path to wisdom. Meanwhile, those
who walk in God's wisdom enjoy God's peace even
on high seas and under turbulent skies.

God's peace can quiet our adversaries. It's
really sad how quickly issues can polarize people—
whether those issues are social, political, or religious.
Although our faith may be one of those potential
hot buttons, we can ask God to show us how to be
people of peace even as we maintain our integrity as
his followers. "When the ways of people please the
Lord, he causes even their enemies to be at peace
with them" (Proverbs 16:7). When we seek to please
our Lord Jesus first and foremost, God wants us to
know that he will come to our aid with his prevailing
peace when we allow him to control our behavior.

Jesus is the Prince of Peace. "A child has been born for us, a son given to us," said Isaiah. "And he is named Wonderful Counselor, Mighty God, Everlasting Father, Prince of Peace" (Isaiah 9:6). This beautiful verse is often read at Christmastime by those who acknowledge Jesus as the Christ. Isaiah's words remind us that Jesus came to make peace between God and humanity—something no one else could have accomplished. That's why Jesus alone is worthy to bear the magnificent title Prince of Peace.

A mind in tune with God's Spirit brings peace. "Those who live according to the Spirit set their minds on the things of the Spirit. To . . . set the mind on the Spirit is life and peace" (Romans 8:5–6). So how can we set our minds on the things of the Spirit? One way is by spending time in the Bible—reading, studying, and memorizing, for God's Spirit always works in agreement with God's Word. Another way is to stay tethered to God in prayer throughout the day. Two mainstays of faith—Scripture and prayer—keep our minds in tune with God's Spirit.

Focusing on God brings peace of mind. Our inner landscape shows on the outside: Worriers tend to fidget, angry people often scowl, and happy people typically smile and laugh. It has a lot to do with where we let our minds camp out. That's why it's good to remember to keep our thoughts moving toward God. "Those of steadfast mind you keep in peace," Isaiah said to the Lord, "in peace because they trust in you" (Isaiah 26:3). As we fix our thoughts on God, we enjoy peace of heart and mind, and that peace will make a difference in the world around us as well.

The future of God's people is a peaceful home. "My people will abide in a peaceful habitation, in secure dwellings, and in quiet resting places," said the Lord (Isaiah 32:18). This passage has a present and future aspect to it. In this world, God himself is our refuge—our secure resting place in an insecure and dangerous world. There is a permanent dwelling place, however, that he's preparing for us where we will live with him in perfect peace one day, far from the difficulties of life in a fallen world. Heaven is our true home—a secure dwelling for all eternity. It is a place where we can forever rest in peace with those who love the Lord and who are deeply loved by the Lord.

The gospel is a message of peace. Can you remember when you first heard the good news of God's reconciling love? Who told you about it? The Scriptures have this to say about those who herald the gospel: "How beautiful upon the mountains are the feet of the messenger who announces peace, who brings good news, who announces salvation" (Isaiah 52:7). Beautiful feet may not seem like much of a compliment, but from a poetic standpoint, it's a lovely tribute to those who carry the gospel message of peace in their hearts and tell it joyfully to others.

Those who trust in Christ have peace with God. What a relief that we're not trying to be justified before God by doing enough good deeds to outweigh our bad deeds! Who could have any certainty of salvation and heaven that way? "Since we are justi-fied by faith, we have peace with God through our Lord Jesus Christ" (Romans 5:1). Thankfully, we're justified by faith in Christ, who paid the price for our sins. There is no scale, only a cross by which we find our peace with God.

Those who work for peace will enjoy the fruits of their labor. Working for peace can be a lot like growing a crop. Our first efforts may seem as though the dark earth has swallowed the seeds of peace without any evidence of growth. Still, we tend that ground, infused with hope for much fruit, and though it may take longer than we ever imagined, there will come a day when our work will pay off and we'll rejoice in a well-deserved harvest. "A harvest of righteousness is sown in peace for those who make peace" (James 3:18). Have you planted some seeds of peace? Don't give up on them!

Christ offers peace in all circumstances. Jesus is no Pollyanna. He knows that there are people and circumstances that will bring trouble into our lives. But he knows, too, that despite these adversities, his peace is available to us in each difficulty. "I have said this to you, so that in me you may have peace," Jesus assures us. "In the world you face persecution. But take courage; I have conquered the world!" (John 16:33). Jesus also reminds us that his victory over darkness will be fully realized when time comes to a close and our eternity with him begins.

There is joy in being in God's presence. There's no other place we find joy in its fullness, shimmering in all its facets, except in the presence of God himself. "You show me the path of life," said the psalmist. "In your presence there is fullness of joy; in your right hand are pleasures forevermore" (Psalm 16:11). We can try manufacturing our own versions of joy by pursuing some of life's temporary pleasures—achievements, recreation, entertainment, material possessions, and such. But these don't come close to the rare joy we experience when we draw close to our heavenly Father so we can spend time in his holy presence.

Joy will always return to those who love God.
We may find ourselves brought low by some of life's difficulties—and certainly by the tragedies that take us by storm. But none of these—not even the tragedies—can rob us of the deep-seated joy we have in our God. "Weeping may linger for the night, but joy comes with the morning" (Psalm 30:5). We may weep, even as Jesus did at times, but like him, we have a future joy set before us that no struggle on this earth can undermine or destroy. Our morning lies just ahead.

Gratitude to God should be filled with joy.
Have you ever felt so thankful to the Lord that you just had to shout your praise out loud or let out a primal whoop for pure joy? "Clap your hands, all you peoples," said the psalmist. "Shout to God with loud songs of joy" (Psalm 47:1). Certainly those expressions are just as fitting as a formal prayer, a hymn, or a chorus of praise. If our children, much to our delight, dance for joy when they open their gifts at Christmastime, surely our heavenly Father wants you to know that he loves to see his children's most authentic expressions of delight at his own gifts

of love. So let us give joyful praise to the one who delights in always blessing us.

Walking uprightly brings joy. Doing things God's way is like walking on a sunlit path where light and delight prevail. "Light dawns for the righteous, and joy for the upright in heart" (Psalm 97:11). It's like the title of that upbeat song that gets so much airtime in the summer: "Walking on Sunshine." That's what it's like to be in open fellowship with God with no shadows of hidden wrongdoing lingering or lurking about. There's the light of righteousness dawning all around us and the joy of God's fellowship lighting our hearts within.

Fitting words bring joy. When you hear someone speak insightfully or you're there when a person says just the right words in a difficult situation, there's a sense of deep satisfaction. You may even feel like shouting, "Good answer!" You'll probably revisit the moment in your thoughts later and note the remark for possible future use. "To make an apt answer is a

joy to anyone, and a word in season, how good it is!"
(Proverbs 15:23). The joy of an apt reply is sweet and
lingers long after the words are spoken.

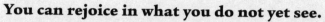

You can rejoice in what you do not yet see.
When Jesus met with his disciples after his resurrection, Thomas's doubts were finally allayed when he
saw and touched the risen Christ for himself. Jesus
then stated that those who believe in him even without seeing will be especially blessed. That includes
you! "Even though you do not see him now," said
the Apostle Peter, "you believe in him and rejoice
with an indescribable and glorious joy, for you are
receiving the outcome of your faith, the salvation
of your souls" (1 Peter 1:8–9). As you wait for Christ's
return, you can rejoice because you have believed
in him without yet seeing.

Joyful noises count as praise. Thankful hearts
are joyful hearts, and joyful hearts seek to give praise
to God. But what qualifies as praise? Do you need a
good singing voice? While singing is one aspect of

praise, thankfully golden vocals are not required. In the Bible's own words, "a joyful noise" is perfectly acceptable tribute to God for the good things he's done. "Let us come into his presence with thanksgiving," said the psalmist. "Let us make a joyful noise to him with songs of praise!" (Psalm 95:2).

There's much to rejoice about. The sink is leaking, gas prices are soaring, and you didn't get the raise you'd hoped for. While such things tempt us to wilt with frustration, we can be glad for food on the table, a roof over our head, clothes on our back; for electricity, lights, running water, warm showers; for good roads, libraries, and postal service. "Rejoice in the Lord always," Paul said. "Again I will say, Rejoice" (Philippians 4:4). Best of all, we can rejoice that we have the freedom to worship, own a Bible, and talk openly about our faith in Christ.

Today's a good day. God wants us to know that today is truly a good day! But what makes today a good day? Did everything go right? (Perhaps it didn't.) Is the sun shining? (It might be pouring rain.) Did your favorite team win? (Maybe they got creamed.) So what makes today a day worth rejoicing in? Good or bad, rain or shine, win or lose, this is the day that God has made. And today we experience his presence. "This is the day that the Lord has made," said the psalmist. "Let us rejoice and be glad in it" (Psalm 118:24). Today *is* a good day.

Kindness is honorable. We're a superstar-studded culture, amused by daily reports of the rich and famous. Standing in a checkout line, scanning tabloid headlines, we're taken off guard when the person in front of us offers to let us go first because we have only a few items. It's a small kindness, but at once we're reminded that some of the most noteworthy people on earth will never glitter in Hollywood's limelight. Instead, their lives shine brightly—and more meaningfully—as they light up the real world with kindness. Indeed, "whoever pursues righteousness and kindness will find life and honor" (Proverbs 21:21).

God saves us because he is kind. There are times when our hard work pays off, and we enjoy the fruits of our own labors. But there are other times when good things come our way as gifts, and we know that they are unmerited. Salvation is one such gift, offered to us not because we deserve it but because the Lord has kind intentions toward us. "When the goodness and loving kindness of God our Savior appeared," said Paul, "he saved us, not because of any works of righteousness that we had done, but according to his mercy" (Titus 3:4–5).

Choosing kindness can be revolutionary.
Kindness has many faces: Compassion, humility, meekness, and patience are just a few of its gentle expressions. With this in mind, each time we're confronted with unkindness, whether it be anger, rudeness, thoughtlessness, or arrogance, we have a choice to make. We can respond in kind, or we can respond with kindness. "As God's chosen ones, holy and beloved, clothe yourselves with compassion, kindness, humility, meekness, and patience" (Colossians 3:12). Be kind and change the world around us!

God's kindness turns us back to him. Sometimes we get headed in the wrong direction in life; at such times, we may want to get back on track or we may be reluctant. In any case, how will God respond to us? With lightning bolts and thunder strikes? What would you say if the answer was "with kindness"? "Do you not realize that God's kindness is meant to lead you to repentance?" (Romans 2:4). It's not a coddling kindness, but a tender mercy that helps us realize we need to turn around and go home—home to our Father's unfailing love.

Choosing kindness can be revolutionary. Kindness has many faces: Compassion, humility, meekness, and patience are just a few of its gentle expressions. With this in mind, each time we're confronted with unkindness, whether it be anger, rudeness, or arrogance, we have a choice to make. We can respond in kind, or we respond with kindness. "As God's chosen ones, holy and beloved, clothe yourselves with compassion, kindness, humility, meekness, and patience" (Colossians 3:12). By choosing one of the many faces of kindness, we embrace God's power to change the world around us.

God calls us to be kind. As God's children, we live and breathe the kindness of God. Each morning we awake to the heartbeat of his tender mercies, and each evening we lie down with the day's blessings lingering within and without. In the wake of this flow of kindness, God is eager for us emulate him by carrying kindness with us into our world, as well. "Finally, all of you, have unity of spirit, sympathy, love for one another, a tender heart, and a humble mind" (1 Peter 3:8). Truly, the Lord wants all of us to be kind to one another.

Patience is better than pride. It's easy to begin something in a fit of self-confidence and excitement, but to finish what we've started in that way is quite another matter. "Better is the end of a thing than its beginning; the patient in spirit are better than the proud in spirit" (Ecclesiastes 7:8). The "long haul" is called that for a good reason; it's an uphill push, a strenuous effort. But a patient spirit will keep putting one foot in front of the other long after the initial excitement has worn off and the real work of accomplishing the goal has set in.

Patience embraces life's learning curves. Have you ever taught a child to spell his or her name, tie a shoe, or ride a bike? It's exciting to watch children keep trying until they "get it." If only we could be as patient with ourselves in the tests and trials and learning curves of life! We'd be in good shape. "Rejoice in hope, be patient in suffering, persevere in prayer," the Apostle Paul tells us (Romans 12:12). So remind yourself today—as life's lessons come at you in their various forms—to be patient with your circumstances, and especially with yourself.

It's important to be patient with everyone. God doesn't discriminate when it comes to being patient with people; fortunately we all get the benefit of his long-suffering nature. Is it any wonder, then, that we're called to refrain from being selectively patient? "The Lord's servant must not be quarrelsome but kindly to everyone, an apt teacher, patient" (2 Timothy 2:24). It's true that some folks try our patience more than others, but as we draw from God's wellspring of love for them, we can keep extending that patient love.

God's people wait patiently for Christ's return. Even when people argue that it's been more than a couple thousand years since Jesus promised to return, we don't need to become defensive, doubtful, or fearful. What we do need to do is remember Jesus' promise. "Be patient, therefore, beloved, until the coming of the Lord," James wrote. "The farmer waits for the precious crop from the earth... You also must be patient" (James 5:7–8). Trusting God's promises can be like waiting for a field of corn to grow; it may take time, but there *will* be a harvest.

God waits patiently for people to turn to him. "The Lord is not slow about his promise, as some think of slowness, but is patient with you, not wanting any to perish, but all to come to repentance" (2 Peter 3:9). In this verse, Peter was responding to people who say, "All this talk about Christ returning has been going on for a lot of years. It's not going to happen." The truth is that God doesn't forget his promises, nor is he ever late in fulfilling them. God is simply waiting, giving people time to turn to him.

Gentleness marks God's people. Gentle people are attractive. We feel safe around them. The children's television show *Mister Rogers's Neighborhood* was popular for many years because its host was the extraordinarily gentle Mr. Fred Rogers (a minister in real life). His show became a sanctuary for people, young and old, who needed a gentle human touch to cheer them along their way. Like them, "Let your gentleness be known to everyone. The Lord is near" (Philippians 4:5). Think of how much sunshine you can then display!

Gentleness is a product of wisdom. "Who is wise and understanding among you?" asked James, who wrote an epistle in the New Testament. He then answered, "Show by your good life that your works are done with gentleness born of wisdom" (James 3:13). Wise children of God perceive the power of gentleness to touch lives and open hearts to the reality of God's love. Thus they waste no time in reaching out to the people around them in gentleness with a listening ear, a helpful hand, a generous gift of time or resources, and a kind word.

Explain faith gently. While faith can be a sensitive topic, if someone asks us about our beliefs, they usually have an authentic interest in knowing our spiritual views. So whenever we explain our faith, we never need to be become defensive; rather, we can gently tell our story. "Always be ready to make your defense to anyone who demands from you an account of the hope that is in you," said Peter. "Yet do it with gentleness and reverence" (1 Peter 3:15–16). Someone once said, telling others about God's saving grace is like one beggar telling another where he found some food.

Warning people requires gentleness. Warning people about sin can be difficult. We may feel torn: First, we're painfully aware of our own weaknesses and shortcomings; yet, second, we see a fellow believer heading for trouble by disregarding God's truth in some blatant way. "My friends," said Paul, "if anyone is detected in a transgression, you who have received the Spirit should restore such a one in a spirit of gentleness" (Galatians 6:1). God wants us to know that the best thing we can do is to pray for them and then humbly talk with them about it, using gentle words from a heart of true concern.

Patience is powerful. As virtues go, patience is the strong, silent type. "With patience a ruler may be persuaded, and a soft tongue can break bones" (Proverbs 25:15). We've all read or watched stories about the quiet patient man who finally wins the woman he's waited for. Or the mother who, through undying patience and love, helps her child overcome seemingly impossible obstacles in order to thrive. Patience, while perhaps underrated as a virtue, is actually very powerful and well worth acquiring. So if you're seeking to grow in patience these days, more power to you!

Waiting for God isn't futile. "What are you waiting for?" people shout impatiently if the first car doesn't move with the green light. Sometimes that's how we feel about waiting for God's purposes to unfold, but God is paying attention. He sees every factor, knows every person, and is working in every heart. "In hope we were saved," said Paul. "But if we hope for what we do not see, we wait for it with patience" (Romans 8:24–25). So we wait patiently, knowing God's light will always turn green and that he will act when it does.

Sometimes it takes courage to wait for God. Sometimes God has us wait until the eleventh hour before he shows us his plan of divine intervention in a situation. At such times, it's a real test of courage to trust him rather than high-tailing it to the nearest escape hatch we can create for ourselves. "Wait for the Lord," said the psalmist. "Be strong, and let your heart take courage; wait for the Lord!" (Psalm 27:14). That courage is a wonderful act of trust and love toward our heavenly Father, one that strengthens our faith as well as our relationship with him.

Self-control in spiritual matters yields eternal benefits. "Keep your eyes on the prize" has been a popular motto for success in pursuing personal goals. But it's even more fitting as an encouragement toward the eternal goals that lie ahead for all who seek God's kingdom. "Athletes exercise self-control in all things," said Paul. "They do it to receive a perishable garland, but we an imperishable one" (1 Corinthians 9:25). People whose eyes are fixed on a heavenly reward practice self-control and make choices that please God, wisely setting aside what's perishable so they can receive what is imperishable.

Self-control brings freedom. Self-control is not letting all our wants and whims call the shots in our life. Because our heavenly Father knows that not all our impulses lead toward good outcomes, God wants us to know that self-control guards us against self-destruction. "The grace of God has appeared," said Paul, "training us to renounce impiety and worldly passions, and in the present age to live lives that are self-controlled, upright, and godly" (Titus 2:11–12). Indeed, self-control is our means for taking flight, as we cast off the fetters of ungodly desires, allowing us to soar on the currents of freedom found in godliness.

Prayer time is the right time to forgive. When you come to the Lord in prayer, it's the perfect time to examine your resentments. "Whenever you stand praying," Jesus said, "forgive, if you have anything against anyone; so that your Father in heaven may also forgive you your trespasses" (Mark 11:25–26). Have you revived an old grudge? Are you planning any revenge? If anything along these lines has cropped up in your mind, it's time to forgive that person who has stirred your heart in the wrong way. Ask God to replace your resentments with his love.

Forgiveness is a way of life for God's people. "Lord, if another member of the church sins against me, how often should I forgive?" Peter asked Jesus. "As many as seven times?" (Matthew 18:21). Peter thought he was being especially forgiving. After all, religious tradition upheld forgiving an offense three times as the standard for magnanimity. That's why when Jesus said, "Not seven times, but, I tell you, seventy-seven times" (verse 22), it stunned him. God wants us to know that forgiveness isn't about keeping track; it's about remembering that we owe our very lives to God's willingness to always forgive us.

God is eager to forgive and restore. Isn't it good to know that God's first desire is to forgive us and restore us? "If my people . . . humble themselves, pray, seek my face, and turn from their wicked ways, then I will . . . forgive their sin and heal their land" (2 Chronicles 7:14). When we get off track, he sees where we're heading and doesn't want us to experience the crash-and-burn outcome of our willful choices. But even though God wants so much to help us, he always leaves the choice up to us, never strong-arming us into his will against our own. Yet he is always present to bring us back to himself.

Forgiveness includes letting go of the little things. Keeping a growing account of the small misdeeds of others in our memory bank is a formula for relational bankruptcy. Accumulating offenses, rather than forgiving them, feeds resentment and anger, and it chokes out our ability to love. "Bear with one another and, if anyone has a complaint against another, forgive each other" Paul taught. "Just as the Lord has forgiven you, so you also must forgive" (Colossians 3:13). Choosing to forgive people is vital for enjoying life and love.

Jesus forgave his enemies. "When they came to the place that is called The Skull, they crucified Jesus there with the criminals.... Then Jesus said, 'Father, forgive them; for they do not know what they are doing'" (Luke 23:33–34). When Jesus asked his heavenly Father not to hold his death sentence against the soldiers who crucified him, he modeled a selfless forgiveness that challenges us to this day. Instead of focusing on the injustice and pain of his ordeal, Jesus forgave those who executed him. So when people hurt us, we are to forgive as well.

Christ's message of forgiveness is to be proclaimed to the world. Children sing, "This little light of mine, I'm gonna let it shine," holding up an index finger like a candle to represent the message of the gospel and the light of Christ in their lives. It can be a reminder to us as well, as we take the light of the gospel into our grown-up world today. "It is written, that the Messiah is to suffer and to rise from the dead," Jesus said, "and that repentance and forgiveness of sins is to be proclaimed in his name to all nations" (Luke 24:46–47).

When we confess our sins, God forgives us.
We never have to run around wringing our hands,
wondering how we can ever compensate for our
transgressions against God. "If we confess our sins,
he who is faithful and just will forgive us our sins
and cleanse us from all unrighteousness" (1 John
1:9). Jesus did the compensating for us on the cross.
Whenever we contritely confess our sins to our
righteous Father in heaven, he immediately forgives
us and washes our soul clean.

Your impossible debt is paid. What if you owed
an impossible debt and had no bankruptcy recourse?
No doubt, you'd be paying on that obligation for
the rest of your natural life. But then what if your
creditor forgave the entire amount? How would
you feel toward that person? You' be overjoyed with
gratitude! Spiritually speaking, God *is* that "person"
in our lives. "If you, O Lord, should mark iniquities,
Lord, who could stand?" asked the psalmist. "But
there is forgiveness with you, so that you may be
revered" (Psalm 130:3–4). What a joy to honor God
for his benevolent love!

The Last Supper is a reminder of God's forgiveness. At the Last Supper, Jesus revealed to his disciples God's astonishing solution to people's sin problem. "Then [Jesus] took a cup, and after giving thanks he gave it to them, saying, 'Drink from it, all of you; for this is my blood of the covenant, which is poured out for many for the forgiveness of sins'" (Matthew 26:27–28). Still today as we drink from the sacred Cup during communion, we remember what Jesus said and receive his provision for the forgiveness we so desperately need.

Only God is qualified to rescue us. Not just anyone can hop in an emergency vehicle and answer a 911 call for help. It wouldn't do any good if a hairstylist or a logger showed up to a heart attack emergency when a qualified paramedic is needed. Similarly, when it comes to being rescued from sin, there's only one qualified to help: God himself. "[The Father] has rescued us from the power of darkness and transferred us into the kingdom of his beloved Son, in whom we have redemption, the forgiveness of sins" (Colossians 1:13–14). In an emergency, God is the one to call.

God's forgiveness is an ongoing blessing.
How many times do we sin in a day? Well, when
we consider that God sees all of our thoughts and
attitudes as well as our words and actions, the
number is quite high. Yet, as we come to God with
humble hearts, recognizing our continual need for
his forgiveness, he extends to us the blessing of his
ongoing willingness to forgive. "Blessed are those
whose iniquities are forgiven, and whose sins are
covered," Paul quoted King David. "Blessed is the
one against whom the Lord will not reckon sin."
(Romans 4:7–8). From the one who committed
terrible sins come the words of assurance of God's
constant forgiveness.

Being kind includes forgiveness. We love being
kind to the people in our lives until they deeply hurt
us. That's when we can almost hear the two-foot-
thick steel door slam shut in our heart. We shut
them out, and we don't want to let them back in.
Oh, how we need to stop ourselves at such times and
remember God's kindness to us! "Be kind to one
another, tender-hearted, forgiving one another, as
God in Christ has forgiven you" (Ephesians 4:32).

In these situations, our first act of kindness should be to forgive, just as he has forgiven us.

Being transparent and accountable is spiritually healthy. We were never meant to be spiritual lone rangers. Fellowship is an important element of a healthy faith walk. God made us for community, so we can grow and thrive in our faith. "Therefore confess your sins to one another, and pray for one another, so that you may be healed" (James 5:16). Do you have people you can talk to about your struggles—people who are on the same path? Keep in touch with them; they're a spiritual lifeline.

Mercy defines God's character. God is first and foremost full of mercy and grace: "The Lord, the Lord, a God merciful and gracious, slow to anger, and abounding in steadfast love and faithfulness" (Exodus 34:6). These are God's own self-describing words that he spoke when he allowed Moses to see just a glimpse of his glory. Likewise God's redeemed children praise his tender mercies and will sing for-ever of his amazing grace.

God's mercy accompanies us through life. As God's children, we experience God's mercy day and night. "Surely goodness and mercy shall follow me all the days of my life" (Psalm 23:6). Mercy opens our eyes to the truth about ourselves and God's love for us. And as we acknowledge that truth, mercy washes over us and puts us in right relationship with God. Then as we walk in renewed fellowship with God, mercy teaches us songs of thanks and praise to joy-fully sing along our way.

God's mercy is a refuge. Baby chicks are known to take shelter under their mother's loving wings. As the hen covers her young, she provides warmth and protection for them. In fact, a prairie hen will cover her chicks when fire sweeps through, and she will perish in the flames in an effort to keep them safe rather than abandon them. "Be merciful to me, O God," the psalmist said to the Lord, "for in you my soul takes refuge; in the shadow of your wings I will take refuge" (Psalm 57:1). God's mercy is like that—self-sacrificing, saving us, and never leaving us alone.

God's mercy brings relief. Sometimes we get ourselves into horrible predicaments. It may be as a result of an innocent mistake, but often it's because we did things our own way rather than God's way. God could say, "I told you so" and turn a deaf ear to our cries for help. But when we admit our fault, he mercifully forgives and helps us get back on our feet again. "Our God is merciful," said the psalmist. "When I was brought low, he saved me. Return, O my soul, to your rest, for the Lord has dealt bountifully with you" (Psalm 116:5-7).

God's mercy doesn't wear out. What if your daily misdeeds were recorded on a chalkboard from the time you woke up till the time you went to sleep? And yet each night before you fell asleep, in repentance, you confessed your sin to God, seeking his mercy and forgiveness. Do you know what your chalkboard would look like when you woke up each morning? That's right: a blank slate! "The steadfast love of the Lord never ceases, his mercies never come to an end; they are new every morning; great is your faithfulness" (Lamentations 3:22–23). Praise God for his never-ending mercies!

God's mercy is for everyone. We like it when the Lord is merciful to *us*, but when other people are behaving badly, we're sometimes a bit too eager to see some form of God's discipline visited upon them. "The Lord is gracious and merciful," said the psalmist. "The Lord is good to all, and his compassion is over all that he has made" (Psalm 145:8–9). Our heavenly Father wants us to know that he loves everyone. He made and cares deeply for those people we believe should receive his harsh judgment. But because he wants to deal as gently with them as possible, his mercy is his first resort with them, as it has been with us.

God calls you to be merciful. "Love your enemies," Jesus tells us, "…and you will be children of the Most High; for he is kind to the ungrateful and the wicked. Be merciful, just as your Father is merciful" (Luke 6:35–36). What a concept to remember! God is kind even to the ungrateful and wicked! It doesn't mean he approves of their attitudes and actions; it just means he isn't mean spirited in return, extending mercy instead. Now here's the challenge: We're called to be just like that—to be merciful even to those who seem to least deserve it.

God's mercy looks through lenses of love. Why on earth would God choose to be merciful to us? Mercy, by definition, means we don't deserve the kind treatment we're getting. So what moves God to be so good to us? Only one thing could: his love. "Be mindful of your mercy, O Lord," said the psalmist. "Do not remember the sins of my youth or my transgressions; according to your steadfast love remember me" (Psalm 25:6-7). And God does. It is from within this unfathomable love of his that he saves us and cherishes us as his own children.

Remembering God's mercy honors him. As we live within God's mercy, we may sometimes lose sight of two facts: (1) Everything good in our lives comes from God; and (2) we literally owe him our lives. "Bless the Lord, O my soul, and do not forget all his benefits—who forgives all your iniquity," said the psalmist, "who satisfies you with good as long as you live" (Psalm 103:2-3, 5). Indeed, it's good to stop and remember how his mercy has impacted us and then give him thanks—an excellent way to honor and bless him for his merciful love.

Merciful people are kind to their animals. We may not always think of how God's mercy flowing through us blesses our pets or livestock, but it does. "The righteous know the needs of their animals, but the mercy of the wicked is cruel" (Proverbs 12:10). The merciful person doesn't stop being merciful just because the beings they're responsible to nurture aren't human. No, their mercy will keep flowing whether they're tending a turtle or a horse. God wants you to know that his mercy in your life even extends to the creatures you care for.

Repentant people receive God's mercy. If we feel we've been too bad to return to God, we need to remember the prodigal son. This disrespectful lad claimed his inheritance early. Then he proceeded to squander it on immoral living. While the father didn't chase after his son, he did wait patiently in hope that his son would return. When that humbled young man finally came home, his father's mercy was unrestrained. "Let the wicked forsake their way, and the unrighteous their thoughts," declared the prophet Isaiah. "Let them return to the Lord, that he may have mercy on them" (Isaiah 55:7).

God knows what he's doing. Sometimes we try to coach God from the sidelines. In our prayers we even make "suggestions" as to how we think God should go about his work. "'For my thoughts are not your thoughts, nor are your ways my ways,' says the Lord. 'For as the heavens are higher than the earth, so are my ways higher than your ways and my thoughts than your thoughts'" (Isaiah 55:8–9). God reminds us that his thoughts and ways are completely beyond ours. That means we can trust him while he works.

Choosing mercy is a victory. When some men brought a woman caught in adultery to Jesus, they were confident that they had trapped Jesus into having to judge her capital offense. But Jesus demonstrated God's mercy not only to the woman but also to her self-righteous accusers. Jesus could have humiliated each man by publicly naming each man's sins, but instead he made his point by saying, "Let anyone among you who is without sin be the first to throw a stone at her" (John 8:7). Jesus was the only one standing there who could have cast that stone, and yet he didn't. Truly, "Mercy triumphs over judgment" (James 2:13). *He silently wrote in the sands the sins of the accusers*

Mercy encourages the weak and weary. Sometimes various factors in life can erode one's commitment to Christ, such as relational struggles, illness, grief, prolonged exposure to faithless environments, compromise, and life in general. "Keep yourselves in the love of God; look forward to the mercy of our Lord Jesus Christ that leads to eternal life. And have mercy on some who are wavering" (Jude 21–22). As fellow believers we can come alongside folks who are struggling and reach out to them, encouraging them with God's mercy and gently reminding them that there are far better things still ahead.

God's mercy is truly worth celebrating. Have you ever thought of establishing a daily habit of celebrating the mercy of God in your life? It could be as simple as picking a flower each day as a joyful reminder of God's mercy, or it could be raising your coffee cup toward heaven before you take your first sip. It could be singing a song in the shower, or it could be writing a line of poetry in your journal. Or you could recite this verse: "Blessed be the God and Father of our Lord Jesus Christ! By his great mercy he has given us a new birth into a living hope" (1 Peter 1:3). Whatever you do, the Lord welcomes every form of gratitude. He wants us to be appreciative of all that he has done for us.

You can give God's comfort to others. The Lord's compassion is always overflowing toward us and through us. "Blessed be . . . the Father of mercies," said Paul, "who consoles us in all our affliction, so that we may be able to console those who are in any affliction" (2 Corinthians 1:3–4). It's something like "pay it forward" when it comes to comforting others. We know how it feels to need consolation, and we know what it's like to receive it from God, either directly or through others. So after having been comforted ourselves, how fitting it is for us to reach out with God's compassion to help people in their time of need!

God provides spiritual armor for spiritual battles. Whenever our commitment to following God is challenged in some way, we have a spiritual battle on our hands. These battles often present themselves through circumstances, situations, or even people, but their outcome is always determined by our own choices. "Be strong in the Lord and in the strength of his power," said Paul. "Put on the whole armor of God, so that you may be able to stand against the wiles of the devil" (Ephesians 6:10–11). When we choose God's strength, using armor he provides, we will always be victorious.

Truth is spiritual armor. Among God's provisions for standing strong in our wholehearted commitment to him is truth. "Stand therefore," said the Apostle Paul, "and fasten the belt of truth around your waist" (Ephesians 6:14). Like a belt that holds other armor in place and on which weaponry is carried, truth is of central importance in our defense against our enemy, the devil, who loves to deal in lies and half-truths in his attempts to undermine our integrity and our faith in the Lord. Practicing truthfulness in our everyday interactions keeps us sharp and ready for spiritual battle.

Being ready to share the gospel is spiritual armor. Our readiness to tell others about God's love and our salvation are like a good pair of military footwear. "As shoes for your feet put on whatever will make you ready to proclaim the gospel of peace" (Ephesians 6:15). Wherever we go, whatever we're doing, when we're ready for opportunities to share the gospel, we're letting others know that they can know victory in their lives by trusting the risen Christ.

Righteousness is spiritual armor. Did you know that *Satan* means "accuser"? Yet, when we're walking in God's ways, clothed in the righteousness of our Savior, none of Satan's accusations can reach our heart. That's why righteousness is like a bullet-proof vest in spiritual battle. Your defense against Satan's taunts and charges of moral failure must always be this: "God has forgiven me and given me the righteousness of Christ as my own." Therefore, "Put on the breastplate of righteousness" (Ephesians 6:14). When you wear his righteousness, you're invulnerable to Satan's accusations.

Faith is spiritual armor. Lies and accusations aren't the only weapons our enemy, the devil, uses against us. He also can be extremely cruel when he attacks our faith. That's why we can't afford to display our faith shield only at church services and mealtime prayers. "With all of these, take the shield of faith, with which you will be able to quench all the flaming arrows of the evil one" (Ephesians 6:16). We need to have that shield well oiled, always at hand, and ready for absolutely anything.

Salvation is spiritual armor. Headgear is indispensable in battle, and this vital piece of physical armor corresponds spiritually with our salvation. Therefore, "Take the helmet of salvation" (Ephesians 6:17). So why is our salvation such an important piece of spiritual armor for us when our faith in Christ is tested? We wouldn't be spiritually alive at all without it! And while we may become wounded from time to time in spiritual battle, our enemy cannot deliver a fatal blow to our spiritual life as long as salvation is in place—for Christ has saved us.

God's Word is spiritual armor. "Take … the sword of the Spirit, which is the word of God" (Ephesians 6:17). This is our spiritual weapon with which we can defeat our enemy. It's what Jesus used when he was tempted in the desert. But be careful! Satan likes to use Scripture, too, taking it just enough out of context to make it sound right, but, in reality, making it all wrong. That's why knowing your weapon (studying Scripture) and knowing how to use it (walking in its truth) are essential to spiritual victory.

Prayer is spiritual alertness. Praying on a continual basis keeps us spiritually alert. "Pray in the Spirit at all times in every prayer and supplication," said Paul. "To that end keep alert and always persevere in supplication for all the saints" (Ephesians 6:18). Does that mean we need to scoot around on our knees 24/7? Not at all. But ongoing prayer is a great way to keep us mindful of our need for God's help.

Prayer is talking with our heavenly Father. Jesus taught, "Pray then in this way: Our Father in heaven, hallowed be your name" (Matthew 6:9). When our children come to us with their heartfelt concerns, we're all ears. God is the perfect parent who *wants* us to come to him and tell him about what's on our heart and mind. Of course, we come to him with proper respect for who he is, but we need not be afraid. He's listening to our every word with love.

Prayer aligns our desires with God's. Knowing that God's understanding is perfect and his ways are best, we eventually realize we can trust him with absolutely everything. "Your kingdom come. Your will be done, on earth as it is in heaven" (Matthew 6:10). We may pray for a particular thing, but as we let it go into his hands with "your will be done," we acknowledge that the best possible outcome is what we really want. Still, telling God our desires is important in building a relationship with him, in opening our hearts to him, and in learning to trust him.

Prayer acknowledges that God is our protector. When we pray, asking our God to rescue us from the evil schemes of our archenemy (and we know who that is), we're acknowledging our need for God's protection. "Do not bring us to the time of trial, but rescue us from the evil one" (Matthew 6:13). Our enemy could easily chew us up and spit us out if we had to face him in our own power. But, thank God, we don't have to do that! God is looking out for us, watching our back—and all around us.

Prayer acknowledges God as our provider. Scriptures remind us that God is the one who gives us the ability to "make wealth." That's why Jesus said in his prayer, "Give us this day our daily bread" (Matthew 6:11). Pausing before a meal to give thanks is just one way we can give glory to God for providing our food. But we don't need to stop there; there are so many ways God provides for us and lots of opportunities throughout the day to thank him for them.

Prayer is a time for getting relationships right. Forgiveness is a big deal to God. So when we ask his forgiveness, his Spirit reminds us of any relationship wrinkles that need ironing out in our lives. "Forgive us our sins, for we ourselves forgive everyone indebted to us" (Luke 11:4). Since God has forgiven our huge sin debt, he requires us to forgive others. Does this mean we ignore problems? Absolutely not! But in the process of working on them, we do so in an atmosphere of love that's ready to forgive.

God gives us everything we need to live well. If you've ever gone on a trip with someone who's a good planner, you know how valuable that person's forethought can be. Everything you need is taken care of. Life with God is like that. "His divine power has given us everything needed for life and godliness," said Peter, "through the knowledge of him who called us by his own glory and goodness" (2 Peter 1:3). The Lord has thought of everything we need to live a life pleasing to him, and he gives those things to us fully and freely.

God gives us great promises. God's promises are precious because they pertain to the most meaningful and needful things of our lives. They are great because they are beyond anything we could have hoped for or imagined in their scope and power—and because, without fail, God will keep each one. "He has given us ... his precious and very great promises, so that through them you may escape from the corruption that is in the world" (2 Peter 1:4). In this life when a fortune can be lost in a moment, God assures us that his great promises stand secure.

God's grace provides strength. The Lord said to Paul, "My grace is sufficient for you, for power is made perfect in weakness" (2 Corinthians 12:9). This may seem backward, but it's the most amazing reality: We can be glad about our weaknesses in this life, whatever they may be, because they are opportunities for the power of God to be displayed in us. Humanly speaking, we tend to prefer having all strengths and no weaknesses, but in Christ Jesus, as we are willing to bring our weaknesses to him, we become mighty in the grace and strength he alone can provide to us.

God rescues the oppressed. Martin Luther King Jr.'s leadership in the civil rights movement was splendid. His powerful speeches, the peaceful protests he prompted, and the faith-filled anthem, "We Shall Overcome," still resound in our consciousness as we lament the wrongs of past oppression and move forward in hope toward unity. The ultimate triumph of King's heroic life reveals that God still fights for the oppressed. "O Lord, who is like you?" asked the psalmist. "You deliver the weak from those too strong for them, the weak and needy from those who despoil them" (Psalm 35:10).

God's strength is a source of joy. The 1981 movie *Chariots of Fire* portrayed Scotland's Eric Liddell's gold-medal race in the 1924 Olympics. Believing his swiftness and strength were from God, Liddell said that when he ran, he felt God's pleasure. The humble athlete's races were for him an exuberant praise to God for the strength God had given him. "Be exalted, O Lord, in your strength!" exclaimed the psalmist. "We will sing and praise your power" (Psalm 21:13). God manifests his strength in many ways, within us and beyond us. Each display is a source of joy and opportunity for praise.

God's strength is a refuge. "From the end of the earth I call to you, when my heart is faint. Lead me to the rock that is higher than I" (Psalm 61:2). Often the "end of the earth" from which we're calling to God is actually the "end of our rope" after we've tried figuring things out on our own, doing them in our own way while relying on our own strength. It's at these times we begin to call on God, seeking refuge in *his* strength. And that's when our dangling feet find their footing again on the solid rock.

Thanksgiving honors God. Thanksgiving isn't just a holiday—it's a way of life for those who love God. "Those who bring thanksgiving as their sacrifice honor me," said the Lord (Psalm 50:23). Even on our worst days, we have much to thank God for. If you're out of practice or just having a tough time being thankful for some reason, here's a challenge: Before getting up in the morning, name five things you can thank God for; then before going to sleep at night, think of five more things. It's a fun exercise, and it's a way to honor God with your gratitude.

Songs of thanksgiving bless God. Did you know that you can bless God? It's the kind of blessing a child gives a parent when the child draws a picture and gives it as a gift or when the child runs up to show spontaneous affection with hugs and kisses. "Blessed be the Lord," sang the psalmist, "... in him my heart trusts; so I am helped, and my heart exults, and with my song I give thanks to him" (Psalm 28:6-7). Whatever our expressions of thanks to the Lord, we are blessing him in the same exuberant way a child hugs a parent.

It's okay to thank God openly. There's nothing wrong with openly giving God credit for his goodness. It can be as simple as saying, "Isn't that a beautiful sunrise God has made?" or maybe telling a friend about how God answered a prayer, or even telling someone about how God has blessed your life. "I will give thanks to you, O Lord, among the peoples," declares the psalmist. "I will sing praises to you among the nations" (Psalm 57:9). Go ahead; it's okay to openly thank the Lord.

Telling others about God's gifts shows our gratitude. Have you ever given someone a gift and then overheard them telling someone else how much they loved it? It makes you know that they're grateful, and it makes you want to give all the more, not for the accolades but because the person felt blessed by what you gave them. "I will give thanks to the Lord with my whole heart," said the psalmist. "I will tell of all your wonderful deeds" (Psalm 9:1). When our thanks to Almighty God spills over into our conversations, God "overhears" it and is pleased with our gratitude.

You can enjoy all edible things God's made.
In the Acts of the Apostles, God told the Apostle
Peter that the dietary taboos he'd grown up with as a
Jew had been lifted—a symbol of the cleansing power
of Christ's atonement. Later, the Apostle Paul said
to Timothy, "Everything created by God is good, and
nothing is to be rejected, provided it is received with
thanksgiving; for it is sanctified by God's word and
by prayer" (1 Timothy 4:4–5). We may still choose
to abstain from some foods, but what's important
about our eating is that we should give thanks to
God when we enjoy his provisions.

**Giving thanks for answered prayer glorifies
God.** In our prayers, we ask our heavenly Father for
various provisions and blessings, and hopefully we
remember to thank him in the same way the psalmist expressed his gratitude to the Lord: "I thank you
that you have answered me and have become my
salvation" (Psalm 118:21). Of course, expressing our
gratitude to God is something we can always get better at, knowing that our thanks is part of giving God
the glory he truly deserves.

Thanksgiving is a way of life in Christ. Those who have experienced God's saving grace have reason to be truly grateful. That's why Paul made this amazing statement: "As you therefore have received Christ Jesus the Lord, continue to live your lives in him, rooted and built up in him…, abounding in thanksgiving" (Colossians 2:6–7). Christ's abundant blessings will always be worthy of our abundant thanks!

You carry on the thanksgiving of generations. "We your people…will give thanks to you forever; from generation to generation we will recount your praise" (Psalm 79:13). This psalm was written thousands of years ago as part of Israel's hymnody. Consider that throughout the intervening generations, its words have survived to speak to you today. God wants you to know that you are a fulfillment of its declaration that faithful believers will give him thanks from generation to generation.

You can call on God for help. When you're in trouble, whom do you call? For emergencies, it's 911.

For leaky pipes, it's the plumber. For toothaches, it's the dentist. In fact, the Yellow Pages offer contact information for thousands of goods and services. But some things we can't find in a telephone book. Salvation, peace of mind, hope, courage, comfort… for such things we can call on the name of our God. "Our help is in the name of the Lord," said the psalmist, "who made heaven and earth" (Psalm 124:8).

God is a warrior who fights for us. Sometimes we may wish life had a few real superheroes to intervene in human events. Actually, however, we have the supreme superhero in God whose all-seeing, all-knowing, and all-powerful presence guards our lives. "The Lord is a warrior," Moses sang. "The Lord is his name" (Exodus 15:3). While we don't always see God at work, his skills as a warrior are unsurpassed, his timing is perfect, and his justice prevails.

God is the supreme ruler. Some people acknowledge God; others don't. That's one of our prerogatives as free moral agents: We can choose what we will believe and what we won't. Nevertheless, God is always at work all around us, supplying boatloads of evidence for us to weigh and consider. "Let them know that you alone, whose name is the Lord, are the Most High over all the earth" (Psalm 83:18). The supreme ruler of the universe tips his hand at every turn, revealing his power, wisdom, and creativity.

God is holy. We say things like "holy cow" and "holy smoke," but they're just slangs—ironic verbal exclamations for effect. But real holiness...what's *that*? It's as if a sacred hush falls just saying the word. God's holiness speaks to his moral purity and perfection. Anything impure isn't going to make it in his presence. That's why we sinners are wholly grateful for Christ. His purity and holiness are credited to us so we can be reconciled to our holy God. That's why "Our heart is glad in him, because we trust in his holy name" (Psalm 33:21).

God is renowned. It's moving to hear a familiar worship song sung in a different language by a people of a different culture. Wherever the Word of God has gone out, it has touched and transformed the hearts of those who have received its message. "Your name, O God, like your praise, reaches to the ends of the earth" (Psalm 48:10). In fact, the Scriptures tell us that the gospel was commissioned to go out to every tongue, tribe, and nation, and that those who receive it will come from every corner of the world.

God is good. There's a joyful response that's become standard whenever someone says, "God is good!" Maybe you know it already; it's "All the time!" Six words, in total, that say almost everything we need to know about God's character. "Praise the Lord, for the Lord is good," sang the psalmist. "Sing to his name, for he is gracious" (Psalm 135:3). By *good* the psalm writer didn't mean mediocre, but, rather, that God's heart is full of the goodness from which his great grace flows.

God is praiseworthy. What's the most praiseworthy thing you've ever done? Did you head up a fund-raiser in your community to help fight a disease? Did you take in foster children? Did you adopt a pet that desperately needed a home? We do praiseworthy things now and then, but God never stops doing them. "Blessed be the name of the Lord from this time on and evermore'" declared the psalmist. "From the rising of the sun to its setting the name of the Lord is to be praised" (Psalm 113:2–3). God will always deserve our praise!

God is with us. When Matthew wrote the following statement, he was quoting the prophetic words from Isaiah 7:14: "'Look, the virgin shall conceive and bear a son, and they shall name him Emmanuel,' which means, 'God is with us'" (Matthew 1:23). What's the significance of that name *Emmanuel*—"God is with us"? It speaks to what Jesus' life on earth was all about: taking on flesh to walk in our shoes; showing us his love; experiencing our pain; bringing healing and hope; paying our sin debt; and making a way for us to live with him in his heavenly kingdom. That's why the name Emmanuel means so much to those who belong to him.

Jesus is the Messiah. "Jesus did many other signs," said John, "which are not written in this book. But these are written so that you may come to believe that Jesus is the Messiah, the Son of God, and that through believing you may have life in his name" (John 20:30–31). John had a front-row seat to Jesus' earthly ministry for about three years. In that time, John became convinced beyond a shadow of doubt that Jesus is truly God's promised Messiah. It is what God wants us to know as well.

Salvation comes only through Jesus. One of the most important things God wants you to know about Jesus is that "There is salvation in no one else, for there is no other name under heaven given among mortals by which we must be saved" (Acts 4:12). Wow! That's an audacious claim—unless it's the truth. And, of course, it is!

Your reputation is valuable. What would you trade for your good reputation? Hopefully you wouldn't! It's worth more than anyone could give you. "A good name is to be chosen rather than great riches" (Proverbs 22:1). Whether your reputation has remained intact or has been made new (both are gifts from God), always guard it as a precious asset.

Your integrity matters. According to God's Word, keeping secrets is a good test of integrity. "A gossip goes about telling secrets, but one who is trustworthy in spirit keeps a confidence" (Proverbs 11:13). Integrity is being the same inside and outside, being true to your principles no matter who's around. It's not the easiest virtue to develop, but when you walk in it, word gets around that you're a person who can be trusted, and people are grateful to secure your friendship.

Your attitude counts. Attitude is a significant element of your character. We can be behaving rightly, but if we have a bad attitude, it actually negates the value of whatever it is we're doing. "Do all things without murmuring and arguing," Paul said, "so that you may be blameless and innocent, children of God" (Philippians 2:14–15). Sometimes we may be required to do something we don't like, but if we choose to do it without complaining, what a difference it can make!

Being good to yourself is important. When Jesus taught that we should love our neighbors as ourselves, he assumed a proper self-love based in God's love for us. "Those who are kind reward themselves, but the cruel do themselves harm" (Proverbs 11:17). If we find ourselves struggling to love others, we can begin by examining how we're viewing and treating ourselves. When we are kind and gentle with ourselves, it almost certainly follows that genuine love will flow from us to those around us. So let God's love in, and be good to yourself!

Being good to others brings joyful satisfaction. As God's love flows through us to those around us, there's a wonderful sense of joyful satisfaction that arises in our hearts. "Happy are those who are kind" (Proverbs 14:21). Of course, it's not a smug self-satisfaction, but rather the peaceful joy that comes from seeing them thrive under the nurture of God's kindness and encouragement, the happiness of engaging meaningfully in relationships.

It's wise to choose words carefully. Have you ever wished you could take back something you just said? Sometimes our words can get us into unexpected trouble or just be plain embarrassing. That's why the rule of thumb in most cases is "The less said, the better." "Those who guard their mouths preserve their lives; those who open wide their lips come to ruin" (Proverbs 13:3). When we speak, we do well to pause a moment to think—sometimes even to pray— before we let the words out.

Financial self-discipline pays off. "Wealth hastily gotten will dwindle, but those who gather little by little will increase it" (Proverbs 13:11). People who are good at saving money will tell you that it's a process that takes intentionality, self-discipline, and patience. And while there are no guarantees in life when it comes to money, when we commit our finances to God's care, we can trust him with our every penny.

It's wise to keep your cool. When we drive in traffic, the smallest slowdown can seem like a major annoyance to us. That's why God wants us to take a deep breath and step back when something disagreeable occurs. "Whoever is slow to anger has great understanding, but one who has a hasty temper exalts folly" (Proverbs 14:29). Keeping your cool can make the difference between a regrettable response and a smart one.

You can be good without being naïve. There's sometimes an impression that being a person of faith means checking your brain at the door, but that's not what Jesus taught his followers. He told them to be shrewd as serpents yet innocent as doves. The Book of Proverbs makes this observation about being thoughtful: "The simple believe everything, but the clever consider their steps" (Proverbs 14:15).

Honoring God brings success. If you discovered that there was someone who knew what the weather was going to be tomorrow, what the stock market was going to do, who was going to win the next presidential election, and where your lost keys were hiding, wouldn't you want that person to be in charge of your life? Well, there is one who can foresee everything, and that one is the supreme Lord of the universe. "Commit your work to the Lord, and your plans will be established" (Proverbs 16:3). When we honor him by entrusting our lives to him, he will faithfully guide us in all our endeavors.

God sees everything. "The eyes of the Lord are in every place, keeping watch on the evil and the good" (Proverbs 15:3). This can be a scary thought if you're not living on the up and up. But God's people can take great comfort in this truth: God sees and doesn't forget. Whenever we do what's right, God sees. Whenever we honor God, he remembers. When we do something good for someone and no one else notices, God does. And on the day of reckoning, he'll bring every hidden thing to light.

God's love is like no other love. "If my father and mother forsake me, the Lord will take me up" (Psalm 27:10). This verse may sound as though God's love is something a person might have to settle for under certain circumstances, but God's love is no mere consolation prize. It's just the opposite: His love is the grand prize—the best of all loves. We know it the moment we lean into it and find the most profound sense of worth and belonging we've ever known. God wants us to know that there's no other love that can support us as his love does.

God's love quiets you. God's love soothes frazzled hearts and minds better than a trip to the spa or any medication. "I have calmed and quieted my soul, like a weaned child with its mother," said the psalmist (Psalm 131:2). Next time you're pulling your hair out (or you feel like pulling out someone else's), find a quiet place, close your eyes, and settle your mind on the reality of God's love for you. Wrap your arms around yourself and say, "No matter what, God loves me." If you truly believe those words, God's inner peace will surely come to you.

God's love nurtures you. From your earliest moments, God's love has nurtured your life. "Upon you I have leaned from my birth," said the psalmist; "it was you who took me from my mother's womb. My praise is continually of you" (Psalm 71:6). God is at work on the unique masterpiece that's you, causing you to grow, develop, and have an awareness of his presence with you. To this day the Lord nurtures you with his love—even now as you hear his Spirit say to you, "My child, how I love you!"

God's love watches over you. Do you ever feel vulnerable and needy? The following verse highlights God's care over the lives of those who most need his protection and provision, but it's not an exhaustive list: "Father of orphans and protector of widows is God in his holy habitation. God gives the desolate a home to live in; he leads out the prisoners to prosperity" (Psalm 68:5–6). God sees your personal vulnerabilities—the places where you feel your greatest need for his love, his protection, and his provision. He sees, and he's watching over you.

God's love is compassionate toward you. Did you grow up with compassion around you? Did you grow up without much? It's easier for some to relate to the idea of God's compassion than it is for others. But our relative experience doesn't change the reality of God's sympathetic love. "As a father has compassion for his children, so the Lord has compassion for those who fear him" (Psalm 103:13). Our heavenly Father comes to us offering kindness, mercy, forgiveness, and a new life. Such tenderness can be surprising if a gentle touch is unfamiliar, but it's a wonderful thing to get used to.

Behind God's discipline is his love for us. Ah, the gentle taps of our good shepherd's staff. At times God's discipline seems like intrusions on our blissful pursuit of some off-the-track object. But those sidetracks lead toward things like cliff edges and raging rivers. So God's nudges—they're love taps, and we need them. "My child, do not despise the Lord's discipline or be weary of his reproof, for the Lord reproves the one he loves, as a father the son in whom he delights" (Proverbs 3:11–12).

God loves to give good things to us. It's helpful to come back to the idea of parenting when we begin to fear God might be out to get us. We can ask ourselves, *Are we out to get our own children?* Of course not! In fact, just as we like to give good gifts to our children, so God enjoys blessing us with good things. "If you then," Jesus said, "know how to give good gifts to your children, how much more will your Father in heaven give good things to those who ask him!" (Matthew 7:11).

God's love strengthens us to do what's good. Keeping our chin up, taking the high road, and choosing to do the next right thing isn't always easy. That's why we always need God's love filling up our tank for the next stretch of high road in front of us. "Now may our Lord Jesus Christ himself and God our Father, who loved us . . . , comfort your hearts and strengthen them in every good work and word" (2 Thessalonians 2:16–17). Spending time each day—even many times a day—touching base with God gives us what we need for "every good work and word."

Because of God's love for us, he will bring us to his home. "In my Father's house there are many dwelling places. If it were not so, would I have told you that I go to prepare a place for you?" Jesus said to his beloved disciples. "I will come again and will take you to myself, so that where I am, there you may be also" (John 14:2–3). What a promise! Our Lord is preparing a place for his loved ones. And he won't make us try to find it with an internet map. No, he's coming to escort us there himself—to show us around our new heavenly home.

God's love will make you glow. Few people know that the final stanza of "Amazing Grace" was added some years after the original five. John Rees penned these stirring words of stanza 6, which look ahead to heaven: "When we've been there ten thousand years, / Bright shining as the sun, / We've no less days to sing God's praise / Than when we've first begun." It *is* amazing to consider—that the same love that saved us will one day make us eternally resplendent. "Then the righteous will shine like the sun in the kingdom of their Father" (Matthew 13:43).

God desires unity within our families. Our relationships with family members or our spiritual brothers and sisters in Christ are meant to be blessings in our lives. God designed family for our mutual benefit—for love, nurture, belonging, fellowship, and support. Families that value each member in an atmosphere of mutual respect enjoy all these benefits, as well as unity. "How very good and pleasant it is when kindred live together in unity!" (Psalm 133:1). Unity is the crowning joy of our love for each other, which is God's design and his desire for our family relationships.

Authentic unity takes effort. "Lead a life worthy of the calling to which you have been called," said Paul, "making every effort to maintain the unity of the Spirit in the bond of peace" (Ephesians 4:1, 3). Anything worth having requires effort on our part, and unity is no exception. We may see a happy family and admire their closeness, but ask them if they ever have conflict, and they'll tell you that it does happen. The key is they don't view differences as reasons for rifts and grudges but as challenges by which to grow in understanding, respect, and love for one another.

God's people are united in his Son. As God's people, our unity isn't found in causes, ministries, or leadership personalities but only in our common faith in Christ Jesus. Any other thing around which we may try to rally will only cause unity to unravel. "The gifts he gave were . . . for building up the body of Christ, until all of us come to the unity of the faith and of the knowledge of the Son of God" (Ephesians 4:11–13). As we keep it all about Christ and his gospel, we'll be able to stand strong together in his truth and love.

Christian unity focuses on our common faith. Faith in Christ unifies God's people and gives us a common purpose; as one body, we live to honor our Lord and tell others about his gospel. So when something divisive arises within our fellowship, we deal with it in a way that honors God and in no way compromises the gospel message. "Now I appeal to you, brothers and sisters," said Paul, "that there be no divisions among you, but that you be united in the same mind and the same purpose" (1 Corinthians 1:10). That's how we preserve our unity.

Unity requires a humble mindset. Within the body of Christ, it's good to remember that our aim is unity, not uniformity. "Be of the same mind, having the same love, being in full accord and of one mind," said Paul. "Let the same mind be in you that was in Christ Jesus" (Philippians 2:2, 5). God made us all different on purpose; he enjoys the variety and individuality among us. So when we adopt our Lord's mindset, we can appreciate the differences in one another—the complementing strengths and weaknesses that make for the loving give-and-take that true unity fosters.

God rewards faithfulness. Beverly Hills, California, and Greenwich Village, New York, may seem like swank neighborhoods from an earthly perspective. But they won't seem like much when God opens his heavenly home and begins rewarding those who have been faithful to him. "I will look with favour on the faithful in the land, so that they may live with me," the Lord promises (Psalm 101:6). Not only does God watch over the faithful, but he also has the best of the best in store for them.

God takes care of the faithful. Those who faithfully follow God enjoy living under his special care. It doesn't mean that they'll never experience hardship, but it does mean that God will see them through it and preserve them from harm. "Love the Lord, all you his saints," said the psalmist. "The Lord preserves the faithful" (Psalm 31:23). God wants us to know that we are never out from under his protection as long as we place our lives into his loving hands.

Faithfulness is a choice. People who marry generally exchange vows; among them is the promise to remain faithful through life's ups and downs—for better or worse, richer or poorer, and in sickness and in health—till death parts them. It's a really huge commitment, but a commitment their mutual love encourages them to make. It's the same way with our choice to be faithful to love and serve God. "I have chosen the way of faithfulness; I set your ordinances before me" (Psalm 119:30). As we commit each day to following him, we choose faithfulness as our way of life.

Faithful people give glory to God. The faithful have learned from experience how wonderful God is—how merciful, how loving, how true, how powerful, how right, and how good! "All your works shall give thanks to you, O Lord, and all your faithful shall bless you," sang the psalmist. "They shall speak of the glory of your kingdom, and tell of your power" (Psalm 145:10–11). No wonder so many hymns and songs of worship have been written by faithful people to give glory to their God!

Faithful messengers are refreshing. In a world of deceptive wording, tricky fine print, and convenient disclaimers, we can become distrustful of what we read and hear. We can't help feeling that most of the messages coming at us from so many directions are false on some level. That's why a messenger of unambiguous truth is refreshing. "Like the cold of snow in the time of harvest are faithful messengers to those who send them; they refresh the spirit of their masters" (Proverbs 25:13). May we ourselves be found faithful as we deliver our master's message!

The faithful pray and are helped. The faithful enjoy the privilege of prayer—of talking to God at any time about anything. What we sometimes forget is that prayer isn't like sending a memo to some cosmic "in-box" for later consideration. Prayer is immediate communication with the living God. Our prayers reach God's ear as we utter them, and he hears and listens. "Let all who are faithful offer prayer to you; at a time of distress, the rush of mighty waters shall not reach them" (Psalm 32:6). Even before we finish praying, our help is on the way.

God enriches the lives of his faithful ones. Our faithfulness stirs God's desire to bless us; it's as if he pulls out all the stops to enrich our lives with goodness. "The Lord . . . stores up sound wisdom for the upright; he is a shield to those who walk blamelessly, guarding the paths of justice and preserving the way of his faithful ones" (Proverbs 2:6–8). Along with giving us protection, granting us justice, and keeping us on the right path, he also opens up the storehouses of wisdom and imparts a generous supply. And there's more . . . so much more!

The faithful can pray with confidence. There's a certain confidence that faithful followers have in their relationship with God. It's not an arrogant self-confidence, but a confident trust in God's love for them. "Vindicate me, O Lord, for I have walked in my integrity, and I have trusted in the Lord without wavering. For your steadfast love is before my eyes, and I walk in faithfulness to you" (Psalm 26:1, 3). We call out to God without hesitation or fear because we know how good he is; we know because we walk in his ways and experience *his* faithfulness.

The faithful will receive God's joy. In Jesus' parable about faithful and unfaithful workers, the master commended the faithful: "Well done,...you have been trustworthy in a few things, I will put you in charge of many things; enter into the joy of your master" (Matthew 25:21). It's a picture of how God will welcome into heaven those who have served him faithfully in this life. To enter into the joy of the master is not just to enjoy his approval, but it's also to be caught up in the perfect joy that fills God's own heart so we feel it too!

The faithful will live forever. "Be faithful until death, and I will give you the crown of life," the Lord promised (Revelation 2:10). This little verse, despite its reference to death, is vibrant with hope and joy. The triumphant ring of "crown of life" is a clarion call, rousing our faith and courage. The promise of eternal life for the faithful unseats every fear, no matter how great, and conquers the uncertainty of death with its assurance of Christ's own resurrection. To be faithful to the end is the great ambition of those who long for life in God's eternal kingdom.

God's Spirit ensures you have the truth. We may wonder how accurate the biblical record of Jesus' ministry and teaching is. "The Advocate, the Holy Spirit, whom the Father will send in my name," said Jesus, "will teach you everything, and remind you of all that I have said to you" (John 14:26). This verse holds the key to trusting that the Gospels contain a true representation of Jesus' words and work. God wants us to know that he sent his Spirit to help witnesses and writers get it right so the world could truly know the Savior.

Remember God today. "Remember your creator in the days of your youth" (Ecclesiastes 12:1). This verse may seem relevant only to young people, but don't dismiss it. Whether you're 20-something or 100-something, you'll never be younger than you are today. That being the case (relative to the rest of your life), today can be considered one of the "days of your youth." So if you've fallen out of touch with the Creator, it's not too late to remember him. He waits to commune with you, to impart his strength, and love to you. Remember him today!

Remember God's track record. When you mull, what do you tend to think about? Your mistakes? Others' offenses? Your to-do list? Your worries? Your problems? Here's a challenge for you: The next time you mull, replace your typical thoughts with thoughts about God's amazing track record—his faithfulness, love, goodness, provision, and protection. Mull on these things and see what happens in your mind and spirit. "I will call to mind the deeds of the Lord," said the psalmist. "I will remember your wonders of old. I will meditate on all your work, and muse on your mighty deeds" (Psalm 77:11–12).

Remember God's ways. There's a whole world out there telling us how to think and live—and if not telling us, then suggesting and pulling us in its direction. It truly takes a conscious effort to remember and choose God's ways. "I remember your name in the night, O Lord, and keep your law. This blessing has fallen to me, for I have kept your precepts" (Psalm 119:55–56). The Psalm writer used the quietude of nighttime to reflect on God and the instruction found in his Word. What are some good times for you when you can recall God's ways?

Remember God in your success. It's a classic human progression: We struggle; we call out to God; he helps us; we feel secure again and begin to thrive and succeed; and then in our success we forget God. Of course, there's nothing wrong with success, but it poses a danger—the danger of leaving God out of our daily equation. "Remember the Lord your God, for it is he who gives you power to get wealth" (Deuteronomy 8:18). Making a habit of remembering God—praying, reading his Word, and fellowshipping with other believers—safeguards us especially in the best of times.

Remember to be charitable. In our little world, we can lose sight of the bigger picture around us. When *we're* not struggling physically, emotionally, or financially, we can forget that there are people out there who *are*—maybe someone right under our nose. It might be a single parent in our neighborhood or church; perhaps it might be someone unemployed or on a fixed income; or maybe it's someone with a disability who could use a hand. "They asked only one thing, that we remember the poor, which was actually what I was eager to do," Paul said (Galatians 2:10). Let us also be eager to do and therefore do!

Remember what you've learned. Sermons, radio preaching, Bible studies and classes, and personal reading and memorization are many ways to receive the Word of God into our lives. Therefore, we should "remember then what [we] received and heard" (Revelation 3:3). But how do we hold onto it so we can draw on it for day-to-day living? Just as in any form of learning, review and repetition are keys to retention. We can also take notes during sermons, order

audio copies of the messages that are especially helpful, and highlight and revisit key passages we find in
our reading. Doing these things will help us recall
what we've learned.

Remember to pray for people. God wants you
to know that he answers our prayers for others, and
here are two ways to help you follow through on
your promises to pray for people: First, if you can
pray right here and now when a prayer need arises,
do so! The best time to pray is now. Second, have a
backup plan if you can't pray in the moment (or if
you intend to continue praying) by right away putting the person's name in your planner (or electronic
calendar). Paul himself said, "Without ceasing I
remember you always in my prayers" (Romans 1:9).
So, like Paul, always pray for the people God has
placed in your heart.

Remember the message of God's love. When
we talk with people, we can fill our conversation

with any number of topics. But the thing nearest and dearest to our heart—the message of God's love and saving grace—isn't always easy to talk about. "Remember Jesus Christ, raised from the dead," said Paul, "that is my gospel" (2 Timothy 2:8). Fear of turning people off by offending them sometimes holds us back. But, despite this fear, we should always remember the very message that revealed our Savior and be ready for the opportunity to talk about him.

Remember you're never alone. After instructing his followers to announce the gospel message throughout the world, Jesus spoke these comforting words to them: "Remember, I am with you always, to the end of the age" (Matthew 28:20). When's the end of the age? When our Lord returns. That means he's with us still today—his Spirit is still guiding, comforting, and helping us along our way. More meaningful than miracles and more enduring than hardship, Christ's own sustaining presence sees us through our days and years until that day when we finally experience the joy of seeing him face to face.

Remember to take time to rest. God set aside one day in seven for us to rest, relax, recoup, and worship. He did it to commemorate his completion of the creation as well as to bless our lives with the regular rest he knew we'd need as finite beings. "Remember the sabbath day, and keep it holy. For in six days the Lord made heaven and earth, ... but rested the seventh day; therefore the Lord blessed the sabbath day" (Exodus 20:8, 11). God set the example for us; he set the day aside and calls us to remember it—that we might be blessed by it.

You are God's good work in progress. God is continually, patiently, and lovingly working out his good purposes in and through you. "I am confident of this," said Paul, "that the one who began a good work among you will bring it to completion by the day of Jesus Christ" (Philippians 1:6). Does that mean he loves you less today than he will on the day that work is complete? Not at all! He loves you every bit as much now as ever. And because of that love, he will persist until every bit of good he intends for you is fulfilled.

Jesus' followers live securely. Following Christ means enjoying the blessings of security and assurance in him. "My sheep hear my voice," said Jesus. "I know them, and they follow me. I give them eternal life, and they will never perish. No one will snatch them out of my hand" (John 10:27–28). As we stay near our shepherd, listening to his voice, we remain fully within his protective care. No spiritual predator can threaten our faith, and no call from another "shepherd" can lure us away from our true shepherd, who alone can lead us to eternal life.

God will hold your hand. For small children, unfamiliar places, large crowds, and dark nights are just a few of the scary things in life—unless a trusted "big person" is close by, offering a hand to hold on to. God knows that even as grown-ups, we still have a good many frightening experiences. That's why he holds out his hand to us, offering his comfort and help: "I, the Lord your God, hold your right hand; it is I who say to you, 'Do not fear, I will help you'" (Isaiah 41:13). Thank God, he is with us at all times.

God gives you enough to share. The generation that lived through the Great Depression has many wonderful stories of how neighbors shared what little they had with each other. It was a time of looking for ways to help those in need. "God is able to provide you with every blessing in abundance," said Paul, "so that by always having enough of everything, you may share abundantly in every good work" (2 Corinthians 9:8). Let us also share what God has given us with those in need.

Children are a gift. Children come into our lives in many ways—if not by our own begetting, then also through our family, friends, neighborhood, and church. "[Children] are indeed a heritage from the Lord" (Psalm 127:3). We hear of their childish antics, funny renderings of language, and unintentionally witty quips, and we can't help but be charmed. One sweet moment in a child's company can redeem ten trying ones. Children's trust, innocence, and vulnerability call out to us for protection and nurture. And in them we see more clearly a reflection of ourselves in the eyes of our Father in heaven.

Everything you say and do matters. When it comes to our lives, there is no reset button or time-out moments in our days. We're "on live" with God 24/7. That's why the Scriptures remind us, "Whatever you do, in word or deed, do everything in the name of the Lord Jesus, giving thanks to God the Father through him" (Colossians 3:17). So as the camera continues to roll on your life, everything you say and do matters, because everything you say and do is an opportunity to grow in gratitude as well as bring honor to God.

It's courageous to wait for God's timing. Your will is twitching. You know you should wait patiently since you're sure God hasn't given you the green light. But you're worried about missing a window of opportunity and losing out on the chance that's passing by. Sometimes waiting takes more courage than charging forward. So if you know you need to wait, stand still and trust God. "Be strong, and let your heart take courage, all you who wait for the Lord" (Psalm 31:24). Be confident in his timing... and in his great love for you.

Contentment is true wealth. In the movie *Citizen Kane,* the main character is haunted by his last memory of joyful contentment. It was from that very moment in childhood he'd been whisked away into an impersonal world of wealth. Despite a lifetime of acquiring and building, Charles Foster Kane could never recapture what he'd lost. In our lives, however, as we trust God to meet our needs, we can realize the true riches of contentment. "There is great gain in godliness combined with contentment," said Paul. "For we brought nothing into the world, so that we can take nothing out of it" (1 Timothy 6:6–7).

God wants to bless your future. The benefits of walking in God's ways are many, but here is one to add to the list: Future generations are blessed when we choose a godly path. "The steadfast love of the Lord is from everlasting to everlasting...," said the psalmist, "and his righteousness to children's children, to those who keep his covenant and remember to do his commandments" (Psalm 103:17–18). Not only does what we teach and model get passed on to our children and grandchildren and beyond, but also

God's own love brings the blessing of righteousness to future generations.

God's promise is for you. It's fun to go to social events where there are drawings for prizes. Inevitably there are those who lament, "I never win *anything*!" Perhaps you feel that way—as if the "prizes" in life don't ever come your way. However, when it comes to the greatest gift—the promise of salvation—God is calling *your* name. "The promise is for you, for your children, and for all who are far away, everyone whom the Lord our God calls to him" (Acts 2:39).

God holds you up. "Our steps are made firm by the Lord, when he delights in our way," said the psalmist; "though we stumble, we shall not fall headlong, for the Lord holds us by the hand" (Psalm 37:23-24). No doubt, this verse brings to mind images of a child learning to walk, held upright by larger, stronger hands tightening gently but firmly around the smaller ones. Our heavenly Father wants us to know that he helps us along in the same way; we may stumble, but he's keeping us upright.

A praying faith in Christ leads to victory. It's a wonderful truth: The smallest act of faith on our part invites Christ's victorious power into our situation. "This is the victory that conquers the world, our faith" (1 John 5:4). One much overlooked act of faith—overlooked because it seems so benign— is prayer. When we pray, we're saying, in essence, "You're it, Lord. You're the one I know can do something about this, and I'm coming to you believing that you will do exactly the right thing at the right time." Prayer, indeed, is an act of victorious faith.

God is for you. It's great to have someone you can count on "in your corner." But can you imagine having God himself in your corner? Well, he is. "If God is for us, who is against us? He who did not withhold his own Son,...will he not with him also give us everything else?" (Romans 8:31–32). God, who is for you and wants to see you victorious in life's battles, gave his own Son's life to secure victory for you. He holds back nothing from you that will help you succeed in reaching your heavenly home.

Faith must remain confident. "Don't look down!" These words are classic advice for the person scaling dizzying heights. It's good advice for us, too, to keep looking up and stay focused on the goal, not on the frightening facts that would rob our concentration and shake our faith. "We are always confident," said Paul, "for we walk by faith, not by sight" (2 Corinthians 5:6–7). We already know the facts, just as the climber knows there are thousands of feet below him and that gravity is pulling in that direction. Focusing on facts, however, won't help us climb. God wants us to know that confident faith will always help us to be strong and courageous.

Faith triumphs over fear. In the Bible, "right hand" is a metaphor for strength, power, and honor.

"Do not fear, for I am with you, do not be afraid, for I am your God; I will strengthen you, I will help you, I will uphold you with my victorious right hand" (Isaiah 41:10). Jesus, the Scriptures also tell us, is seated at the Father's right hand, victorious over sin, death, and the evil. Jesus himself *is* the Father's victorious right hand—the one through whom we are strengthened and upheld. And it is through faith in Christ that we triumph over fear.

Faith leads to peace. When Jesus called his disciples to peace, he asked them to trust in him. "Peace I leave with you," Jesus told his followers. "My peace I give to you. I do not give to you as the world gives. Do not let your hearts be troubled, and do not let them be afraid" (John 14:27). Jesus knew that when we believe that he is in control, our faith would inevitably lead to the peace of heart and mind that no circumstance could disturb. Those first followers kept their peace through thick and thin, and today, so can we. When we place our faith in Jesus and follow his teachings, God places his peace in our hearts and minds no matter what is happening to us.

Don't be afraid of the dark. Darkness symbolizes the unknown and what we fear. And yet, God sees everything that's hidden in darkness as clearly as in the light. "The Lord is my light and my salvation; whom shall I fear? The Lord is the stronghold of my life; of whom shall I be afraid?" (Psalm 27:1). Everything unknown to us and what we fear—God knows it, sees it, and has a bead on it. So, even if we're in the dark, we don't need to be afraid; our Savior is leading the way, and his lantern is full on.

Giving is its own blessing. As children, most of us didn't believe that giving could be better than receiving. Who of us would have forfeited our unopened Christmas gifts to someone else? Sure, after they were opened, we might've parted with the socks and math flash cards, but not the good stuff. Years later we find exquisite happiness in seeing others delight in our gifts. "Remembering the words of the Lord Jesus, for he himself said, 'It is more blessed to give than to receive'" (Acts 20:35). Our maturing love has learned the wonderful secret of giving.

There's no one greater than God. Who are the greatest people on earth? The ones with the most money? The ones with great power? The most famous? The most beautiful? The smartest? The most talented? Make your list, and check it twice. Not one person on your list—not all of the people on it combined—comes close to God's greatness. "Great is the Lord, and greatly to be praised," said the psalmist. "His greatness is unsearchable" (Psalm 145:3). Moreover, if you belong to God, you've got a heavenly Father who's not only greater than anyone but also who truly loves you.

Spiritual strength doesn't depend on physical ability. It's interesting to note that some of the best examples of vigorous faith can be found where physical strength is lacking. Children eagerly tell about their faith. Seniors can be tremendous prayer warriors. And physically impaired believers, such as Joni Eareckson Tada, are some of the most powerful messengers of the grace and strength God provides. "My flesh and my heart may fail," said the psalmist, "but God is the strength of my heart and my portion forever" (Psalm 73:26). Such examples inspire us to stand strong in the Lord.

God's Spirit guides you. "When the Spirit of truth comes," Jesus said, "he will guide you into all the truth" (John 16:13). The Acts of the Apostles records the event at Pentecost, which marked the coming of God's Spirit—just as Jesus had promised to his disciples. It's the Holy Spirit's work in us that opens our understanding to the Scriptures, informs our conscience, and guides us in our decisions. Without the Holy Spirit, we'd be on our own trying to navigate through life. With him, we have the very presence of God within and beside us, guarding our hearts and keeping us steadfast in the truth.